Favourite walks around Oswestry and the Borders

Oswestry Group of
the Ramblers

First Published 2009

Tre Tylluan, Dolybont, Llanrhaeadr Ym Mochnant, Oswestry SY10 0LJ

ISBN 978-1-906494-16-2

Design, maps and production by Jane and Ray Hadlow

Edited by Peter Carr

Cover photographs by Ray Groome

Typeset in Minion and Fruitger

Printed by WPG Ltd, Welshpool

Great care has been taken in the compilation of this publication to ensure accuracy. However, the publishers cannot accept responsibility for any errors that may appear, changes post publication to the footpaths used, or the consequences of errors or changes. If you are in any doubt about access, check before you proceed.

The Oswestry Group acknowledges with grateful thanks the efforts of all members who have checked, walked and re-checked these walks to ensure that they are as accurate as possible.

Introduction

When contemplating walking in Shropshire, most people will probably first think of the Long Mynd, the South Shropshire Hills, Wenlock Edge, the Wrekin and the Stiperstones. However, to the far north-west of the county, the historic border market town of Oswestry nestles against the Oswestry Uplands in an area that has Wales to the west, north and south. The area was once in Wales and still is true border country where many villages in England have Welsh names and Welsh is commonly heard spoken, particularly on market days. It is a very special area, where Wales meets what we think of as 'our forgotten bit of Shropshire'.

This is wonderful and very varied walking country. Immediately to the east of the town lies the relatively flat Shropshire plain, where, in addition to quiet country lanes and a network of field paths, there is ample opportunity for leisurely rambles along the towpaths of the Montgomery, Ellesmere and Llangollen canals. The Oswestry Uplands to the west of the town stretch from Llanymynech Rocks in the south, to Chirk, just over the river Ceiriog into Wales; the long distance Offa's Dyke Path follows the line of these hills. There are some spectacular distant views across much of Shropshire and into Wales from the high points on this ridge.

Then there are the two little-known but beautiful river valleys close by in neighbouring Wales. To the south, the Tanat valley wanders through farming country from the foothills of the Berwyn Mountains. The narrower Ceiriog valley stretches from the village of Llanarmon Dyffryn Ceiriog, deep in the same foothills, downstream to Chirk, and on to join the Dee. Walking up onto the open hills from Llanarmon DC and other places along the Ceiriog will keep you fit and provide wide views of the Berwyns and, on good days, some of the more distant Welsh mountain peaks.

We have compiled this short book of walks in order to introduce ramblers to the very special, unspoilt and quiet, rural places where we love to walk and enjoy the countryside. We hope that you too will soon come to understand why we are so proud of our Oswestry Ramblers' area.

Bob Kimber
Chairman, Oswestry Group, the Ramblers

Location of walks

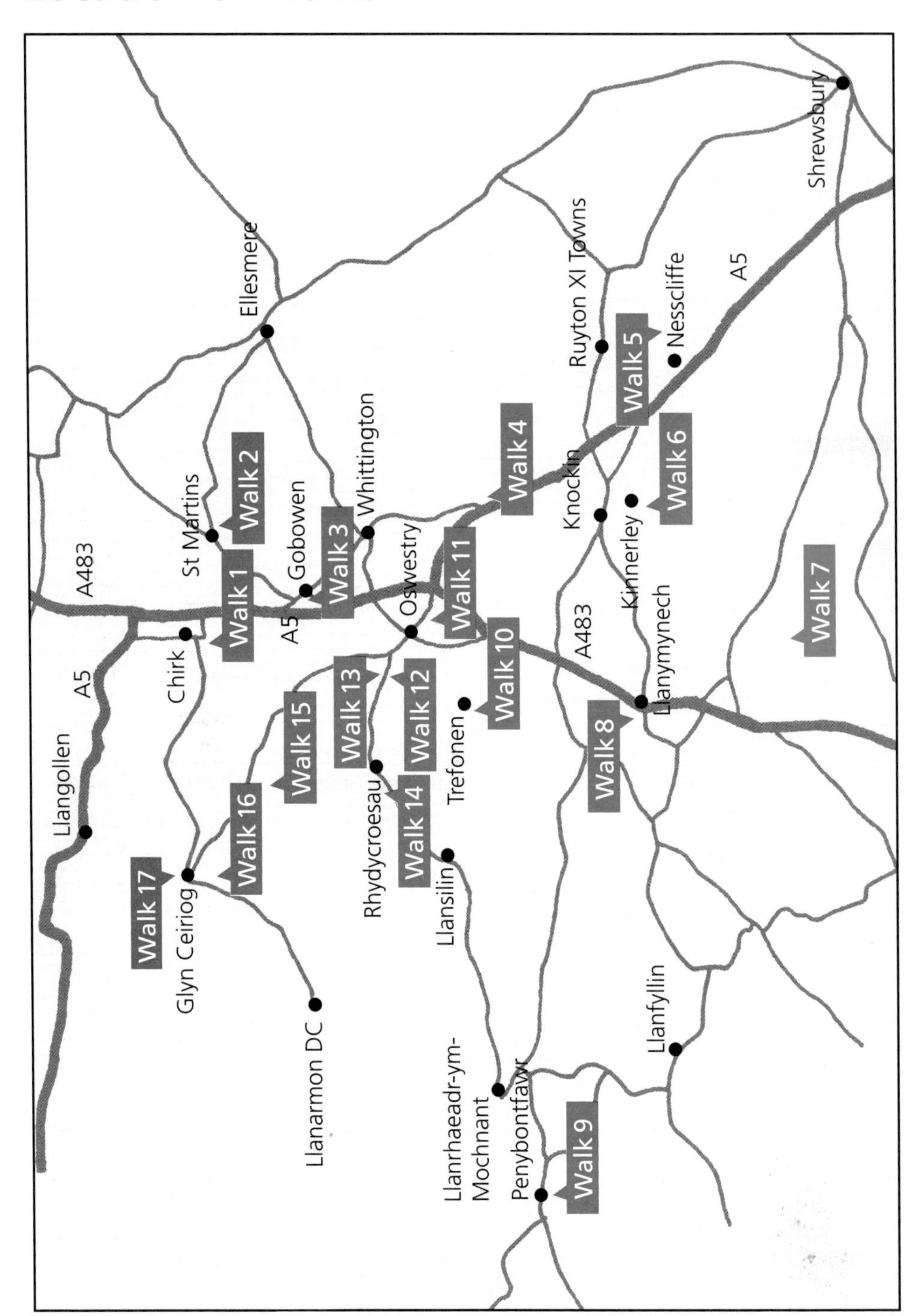

Summary of walks

Walk Number	Brief Description	Start Point & Grid Ref	Distance (Approx)	Grade
1 *(page 1)*	Round the outskirts of Weston Rhyn	Chirk Bank, CP next to the canal – SJ292371	4.7 miles	Leisurely
2 *(page 3)*	A leisurely walk round St Martins	Miners' Memorial Gardens – SJ324368	4.25 miles	Leisurely
3 *(page 6)*	Gobowen boundary walk	All Saints' Parish Church, Chirk Road, Gobowen – SJ302339	4 miles	Leisurely
4 *(page 9)*	A stroll round Haughton, Tedsmore and Grimpo	CP opposite Queens Head public house – SJ339268	6 miles	Leisurely
5 *(page 12)*	Nesscliffe Country Park and The Cliffe	Pine CP just outside Hopton on the Great Ness Road – SJ389318	5 miles	Leisurely
6 *(page 15)*	A scenic walk round Kinnerley	St Mary's Church – SJ338209	4 miles	Leisurely
7 *(page 17)*	Rodney's Pillar	CP near village of Criggion – SJ294148	4 miles	Moderate
8 *(page 19)*	Llanymynech Heritage Site	CP beside Dolphin public house – SJ266209	3.9 miles	Moderate
9 *(page 23)*	Penybontfawr Hill and Forest. Two walks which can be combined to provide a 9.5 mile circuit	Free CP Penybontfawr – SJ088245	4.8 miles & 6 miles Combined 9.5 miles	Strenuous
10 *(page 27)*	The Moelydd	Trefonen Chapel Green CP – SJ260267	4.3 miles	Moderate
11 *(page 29)*	Weston to Morda and back	Queens Road, Oswestry – SJ291291	5.6 miles	Leisurely
12 *(page 32)*	Racecourse to Pant Glas	CP at Oswestry Old Racecourse – SJ259305	5 miles	Moderate
13 *(page 34)*	Racecourse and Candy Woods	CP at Oswestry Old Racecourse – SJ259305	3.5 miles	Moderate
14 *(page 37)*	Rhydycroesau Woods	Large clearing at entrance to woods at Rhydycroesau – SJ241303	3.5 miles	Moderate
15 *(page 39)*	Pen y Gwely from Caemor Wood via Llechrydau	Caemor Wood – SJ220351	4.4 miles	Leisurely
16 *(page 42)*	Teirw Valley & Pandy Crags – two walks	Pont-y-Meibion – SJ196352	6 & 4 miles	Moderate/ Leisurely
17 *(page 45)*	Circles the village of Glyn Ceiriog	Llwynmawr (Golden Pheasant) – SJ225369	6.75 miles	Strenuous

Walk Grades

- **Leisurely Walks** for reasonably fit people with at least a little country walking experience. May include unsurfaced rural paths and fields. Walking boots and warm, waterproof clothing are recommended.
- **Moderate Walks** for people with country walking experience and a good level of fitness. May include some steep paths and open country. Walking boots and warm, waterproof clothing are essential.
- **Strenuous Walks** for experienced country walkers with an above average fitness level. May include hills and rough country. Walking boots and warm, waterproof clothing are essential.

Maps

Note: maps are sketches only and are not necessarily to scale

The Countryside code

- Be safe – plan ahead and follow any signs
- Leave gates and property as you find them
- Protect plants and animals, and take your litter home
- Keep dogs under close control
- Consider other people

Useful Information

Footpath problems in Shropshire
Contact Countryside Service – Shropshire Council
Tel: 01743 255061
Email: countryside.access@shropshire.gov.uk

Footpath problems in the Ceiriog Valley
Contact the Rights of Way and Access Team – Wrexham County Borough Council
Tel: 01978 292057
Email: rightsofway@wrexham.gov.uk

Footpath problems in Powys
Contact Countryside Services – Powys County Council
Tel: 01597 827500
Email: rightsofway@powys.gov.uk

Buses from Oswestry
Traveline West Midlands Tel: 0871 200 22 33
www.travelinemidlands.co.uk

The Ramblers
Membership and any other enquiries:
2nd floor, Camelford House, 87-90 Albert Embankment, London SE1 7TW
Tel: 020 7339 8500
www.ramblers.org.uk

Around Weston Rhyn (including part of the Llangollen branch of the Shropshire Union Canal)

Clive Lagarde

Grade Leisurely
Map OS Explorer™ Sheet 240
Start point Chirk Bank, car park next to the canal – Grid Ref SJ292371. The car park is just by Bridge 21 over the canal and just off the canal towpath which, at this point, is a private access road for properties just along the canal
Distance 4.7 miles (7.6 km)
Ascent Negligible
Duration 2.5 hours
Terrain Field paths and quiet lanes

A leisurely walk round the outskirts of Weston Rhyn, taking in part of the canal towpath, fields and tracks. Provides excellent views of the Chirk Aqueduct.

The settlement of Weston Rhyn dates back to the Doomsday Book. Many of the Victorian buildings in the centre of Weston Rhyn were built as housing for the miners serving the North Shropshire coalfields. Today the surrounding modern housing estates provide homes for commuters.

The area just to the north around the Shropshire Union Canal (Llangollen branch) provides an attractive area for walking and forms the last part of this walk. Chirk Aqueduct, built between 1796 and 1801 by Thomas Telford and William Jessop, carrying the canal over the river Ceiriog, is 70 ft high with 10 arches. Moreton Hall to the south of the canal, once a fine old mansion, is now an independent girls' school.

Directions

1 Cross over the canal bridge and at 100 m turn right through the kissing gate onto the Ceiriog Trail. Go along the path and cross two stiles either side of a track. Continue along the path across to the field edge then follow the fence to the railway (GR 287371).

2 Taking great care, cross the railway and follow the hedge to cross a stile on the right into a wood. Follow the path to reach a minor road (at this point you leave the Ceiriog Trail). Turn left and walk up hill for approximately 400 m to a stile on the right (this is just before a minor road comes in from the left – GR 284367).

3 Cross the stile into paddocks then go up to a stile at 200 m, over the stile and follow the fence on your right through a low pedestrian tunnel to a minor road. Cross the road, go left and go over the stile on the right, then take the path to the left up the hill to the wood. Go through the wood and straight across a field to a stile. (If you look to your left you will see a stone circle; it's not ancient but worth a look.) Go over the stile onto the road (GR 277363).

4 Turn left and walk down to Weston Rhyn where, at the junction, cross over into Vicarage Lane. Continue to the T-junction, then cross over a stile immediately opposite the junction and continue on to a railway crossing (GR 293355).

5 Follow the path over the railway to a five-bar gate. At this point the path follows the fence on the right for 100 m to a stile on your left. Cross the stile and follow the hedge-line to a bridge, then continue over the school grounds to a petrol station (on the A5). Turn left here to pass behind the station and cross a stile alongside the canal. The path leads along the edge of a golf course with the canal on the right hand side, then passes through a small industrial area to a road with a bridge on the right (GR 296362).

6 Cross over the bridge and take the towpath to the left and follow this path back to the car park. Half way along the canal path you will pass The Poacher's Pocket. There is some erosion on the towpath; please take care with children.

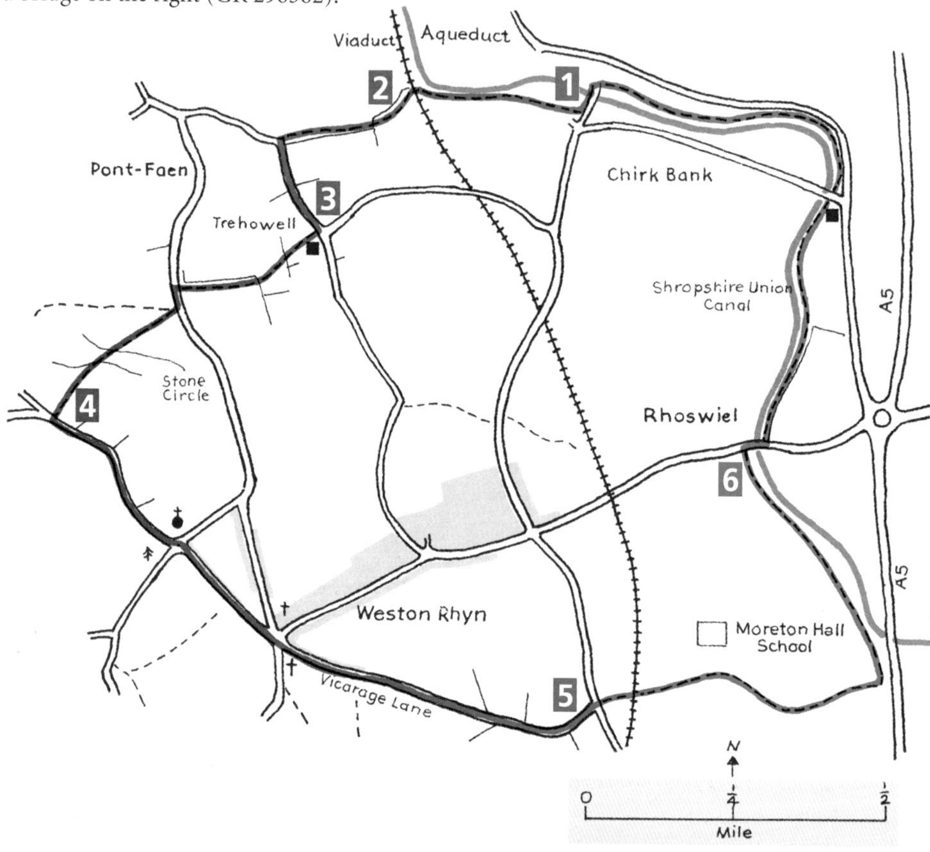

Photo: George Swift

St Martins

Ron Bond

Grade Leisurely
Map OS Explorer™ Sheet 240
Start point Miners' Memorial Gardens opposite Stans supermarket – Grid Ref SJ324368
Distance 4.25 miles (6.8 km)
Ascent Negligible
Duration 2 hours
Terrain Field paths, canal towpath and quiet lanes

A reasonably easy field and lane walk around the former mining village of St Martins, with views across the Shropshire countryside, passing along part of the Shropshire Union Canal (Llangollen Branch), and later dipping into a quiet wooded valley before rising back to the village.

St Martins grew up around Ifton Colliery and the village is shaped by its mining past. Many of the features of the community still reflect this; indeed the start of the walk, 'the Miners' Memorial Garden', is a direct link with that time. There is a small tub of coal mounted on rails in the Garden to act as a memorial to the mine. There is also an imposing miners' social club that was built in 1932. Not surprisingly, the Ifton Colliery was on Colliery Road. The site is now private land, although the office block and the pit head baths remain.

The mine was originally sunk in the 19th century and at its peak employed around 1300 men. It finally closed in 1968 due to underground problems and loss of its markets, although the landscape still reflected the area's heavy industry as recently as 1977. Today St Martins is a pleasant rural village with little of the ravages of mining remaining visible.

Directions

Warning: Step 2 involves crossing a stream and as there is no proper bridge, you have to step through the water; this is usually very shallow but will be deeper in winter or very wet weather.

1 Start at the Miners' Memorial Garden opposite Stans supermarket. Walk south down Green Lane. Pass St Martins church and reach a T-junction. Turn left and in 30 m cross the road to the Pinfold (a pen in which lost animals were placed until claimed; claimants had to pay a fine) (GR 323362).

2 Turn right beside the enclosure and go over the stile. Walk down the field with the hedge on the right and then across an open field due south to reach a waymarked metal gate. Go through the gate and continue south passing or climbing over three small stiles that mark annually erected electric fencing. After the last stile continue downhill to the hedge and a brook. Turn right over a stile and walk 15 m along the bank. Cross the stream and go over the stile into the field (see warning at start of walk description). Continue due south over the low shoulder of a small hill until you arrive at another lone stile at the side of a rotting fallen tree trunk. Pass straight on staying close to the hedge. As the hedge bends to the left cut across the now narrow field to a small post on the canal. Cross a small footbridge to join the canal towpath (GR 323353).

3 Turn right and follow the canal towpath all the way to the first bridge (Bridge 13). The church tower is visible from the towpath. Walk ahead under the road bridge and turn right up some steps (GR 314357).

4 At the top of the steps turn left, towards St Martins, and continue on the footpath up the main road until just before the bus stop shelter (GR 314358).

5 Turn left over a stile and go across a small field and ahead over another stile. Continue in the same direction aiming well to the right of an electricity pole ahead. Then go through a large gap in the hedge where there was once a gate. Continue straight ahead – aim for a large tree – to arrive at a metal gate with a stile on the right. Go over the stile and, with a hedge on the left, continue to a metal gate with an overgrown stile on the right. Go through the gate and straight ahead passing

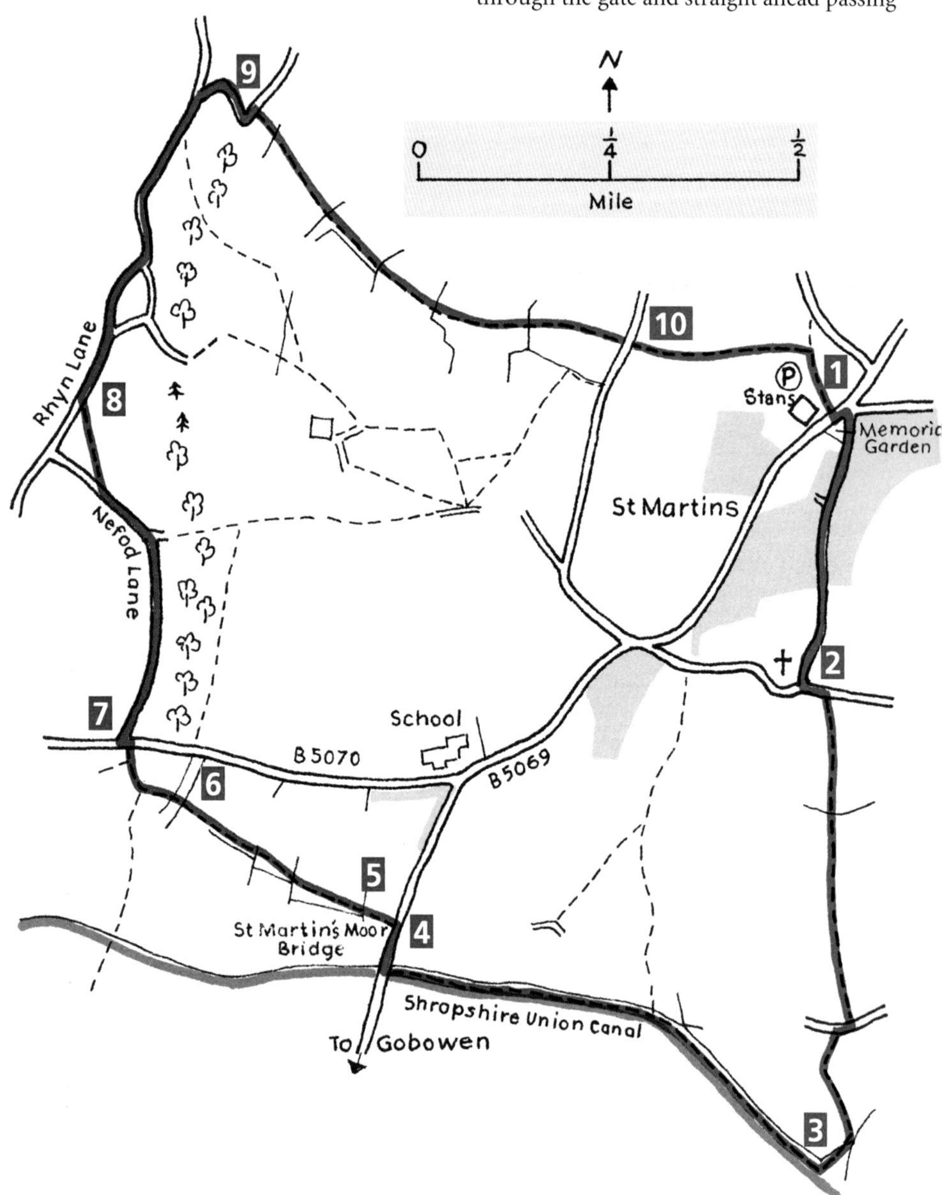

through the embankment of a disused railway (GR 361310).

6 Immediately you reach a further gate with a good stile on the right; go over and then immediately right through a tumbledown gate into a field. Walk ahead slightly diagonally down the field but keeping quite close to the fence. A home-made stile quickly comes into view with an old mill house behind; go over the stile, down the short but steep bank to and over another low stile and down the path to a lane. Turn right and walk approximately 50 m to the main road (GR 309362).

7 Turn left and walk 25 m along the main road over the small river bridge. Taking great care, cross the often busy road and enter Nefod Lane. Go along the lane (due north) – the lane eventually becomes a track which is initially grassy. Ignoring a marked path on the right about 200 m past the last house, walk on round the bend and up a rising earth lane. Continue slightly uphill along the lane. In 150 m turn right over a stile through the hedge. Walk diagonally left across the top of the field to a stile right in the corner; cross the stile into a tarmac lane (GR 307367).

8 Turn right along the lane and continue until you go past a farm called Dungannon, then turn right down a very minor tarmac road on a steep hill. It has a notice 'Unsuitable for heavy goods traffic'. At the bottom cross the bridge with a small waterfall on the left (GR 311374).

9 Turn left after the bridge, then in about 30 m turn right up a wide signposted footpath. The path passes immediately behind a stable and then over a stile into the field. Carry on up the hill bearing very slightly to the right to an easily seen stile to the right of an oak tree. Go over the stile and ahead almost due east with a fence on the right, then over the next stile behind the third oak tree. Go straight ahead to another visible stile, ignore the metal gate 10 m to the right. Go over the stile and head across the field diagonally left to a stile in the fence. Go over this stile and ahead east to the next stile in the hedge. Over the stile again and still on the same line aim for a largish gap in the high hedge ahead. Go up the small bank, over the stile and into a lane (GR 317370).

10 Cross straight over the lane and go over a stile into the next field. Keep ahead in the same direction. Soon Stans supermarket roof comes into view. Aim left to go through a gap in the corner of the hedge line that comes in from the left. Go straight ahead with a hedge on your right to the next stile in the corner; go over and after one small field over a further stile and then one immediately on the right into Stans supermarket car park. Go across the car park to the road and back to the start point.

Gobowen Boundary Walk

Miles Ambridge

Grade	Leisurely
Map	OS Explorer™ Sheet 240
Start point	All Saints' Parish Church, Chirk Road, Gobowen – Grid Ref SJ302339. (Car parking in the two side roads surrounding the church). The church is 350 m from the village roundabout. Buses run every half hour from Oswestry to the village centre
Distance	4 miles (6.44 km)
Ascent	Negligible
Duration	Approximately 2 hours without refreshment breaks
Terrain	Good paths. There are about 10 stiles and two gates to climb over and the A5 and railway to cross.

The walk takes you away from the main built up area into the surrounding lanes and fields. Of special interests are Wat's Dyke, Derwen College Arboretum, Betty's tea shop (well prepared wholesome refreshments at a very economical price) and The Meadows.

Gobowen is a large but peaceful village bypassed by the busy A5. However, before the road improvements, the main London to Holyhead road passed through the village.

Open cast mining was recorded in the area of Gobowen as early as the 12th century.

The village is home to Derwen College for students with disabilities. The Derwen College Arboretum was created out of former farmland about 5 years ago. There is a bird hide that is open to the public – acknowledgement of entrance would be appreciated.

The line of Wat's Dyke (8th century, although the date is disputed) earth works similar to Offa's Dyke but probably older, is encountered twice on this walk (in section 5 and in The Meadows where it forms the eastern boundary). It extends from Basingwerk Abbey, Holywell, Flintshire to Oswestry and then follows the River Morda and ends somewhere near Maesbury.

Directions

1 Starting from the road behind the church, walk south, towards the village centre. After 180 m take a narrow passage on the right. Follow this and cross a footbridge over the railway (Shrewsbury to Chester), cross the field to a gate onto the A5 road (GR 299337).

2 Cross the A5 (very busy – please take care) and continue in a westerly direction into a green lane for a few yards until you come to a kissing gate on the left. Go through the kissing gate and across the field to a gate on the opposite side (GR 298336).

3 Turn left, going south, through/over two gates and past old farm buildings to enter a field. Bear slightly right crossing the field to a stile in the opposite field boundary. Climb over the stile and over a plank bridge. Continue crossing the fields in a generally southerly direction until you encounter a tarmac road (GR 298329).

4 Turn right and after about 45 m climb up left into a narrow strip of wood. Continue in a generally southerly direction across two more grass fields (4 stiles and a plank bridge over a steam) to a lone house – Yewtree Cottage (GR 298327). The fields that you have been passing through are owned by an organic milk producer.

5 Just after the house there is an access lane and just at the start of this is a stile on the left hand side; cross the stile into the field and continue straight across to the hedge line – Wat's Dyke. Turn left and on reaching the field corner with two galvanised gates, go through the first gate and then through the second gate immediately on your right. Turn left for a short distance to the boundary hedge of the A5 road (GR300327).

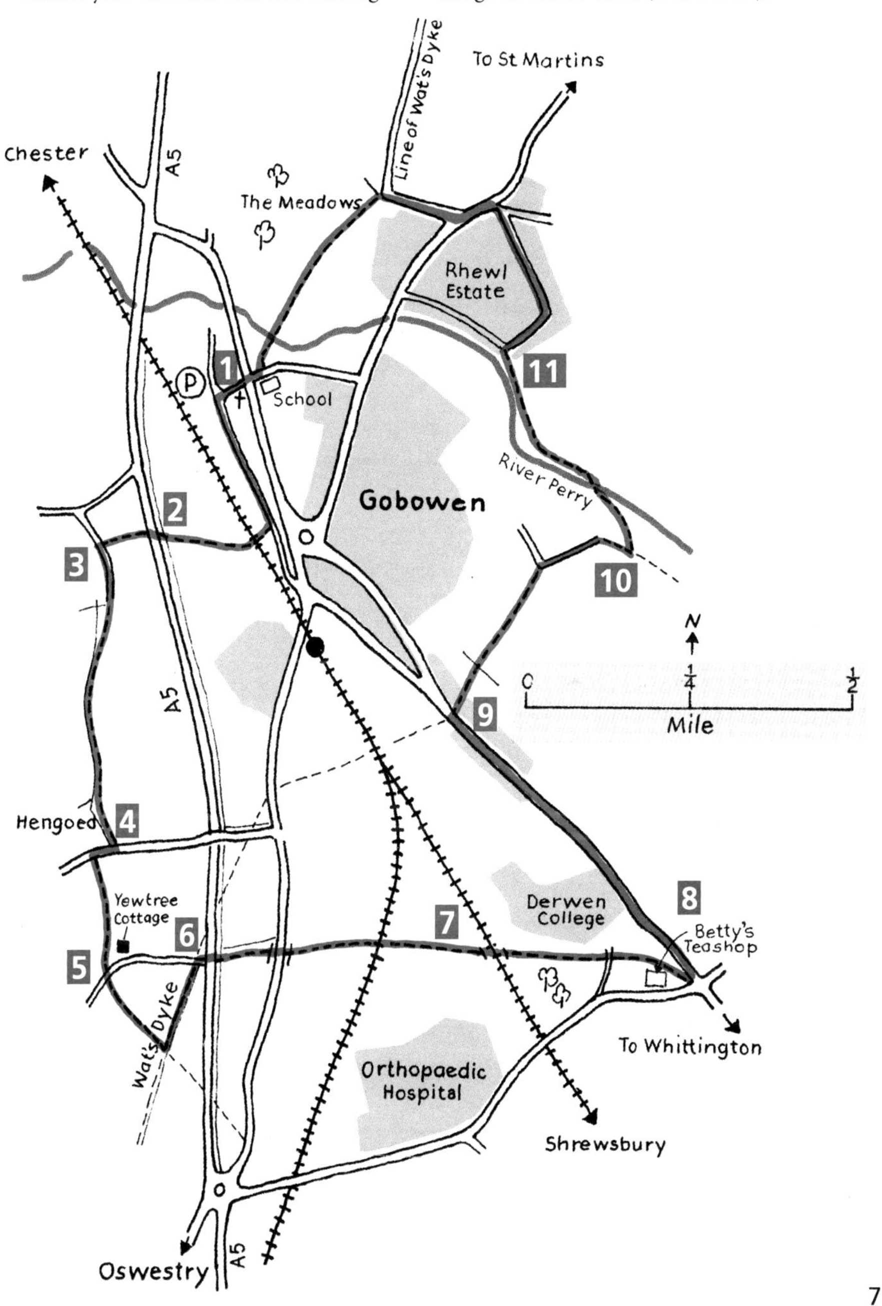

6 Cross the stile onto the A5 and then cross straight over the A5 (as before – please take care). Cross a stile again on the easterly side of the A5 and continue east until you meet the Oswestry–Gobowen road; you will see a blacksmiths/metal workshop opposite. Take the stile at the southerly side of the workshop to enter a field and continue east keeping to the side of the hedge and stream. Cross the obsolete Cambrian Gobowen–Oswestry railway track and continue on the footpath (this is now hemmed in between the stream and the Leylandii hedge at the back of the Meadowbrook retirement bungalows) until your reach the main Shrewsbury to Chester railway line (GR 307327).

7 Take great care and cross the railway track using the steps on either side of the track. You now enter the Derwen College Arboretum. The footpath passes by a games field, horticultural section with its retail shop and on to Betty's Tea Shop (GR312327).

8 Leaving Betty's tea shop, make your way round the bowling green to the boundary corner and onto the Whittington to Gobowen road; turn left along the pavement towards Gobowen centre. After about half a mile (0.8 km), just before the road divides, there is a fingerpost pointing to the right up a passage way (GR 306333).

9 Take the passage way and then enter a field straight ahead. Cross the field and enter a green lane and turn right, continue along the lane to the end. On the right is a farm that has been converted to a rural business (Traditional Products – Joinery) (GR 310336).

10 At the end of the track enter the field and turn left down to the corner. Cross over the River Perry (stream) into the next grass field (this field has a distinct saucer shaped topography). Turn left and follow the hedge to a stile that leads into the Rhewl 'suburb' (GR 308341).

11 Once on the tarmac road, turn right up the slope to the end and go through a passage way into Rhewl lane. Continue along Rhewl lane to the Gobowen–St Martins road. Turn left and then almost immediately right into Preesenthe Lane. At a right hand turn in this lane enter 'The Meadows' via a kissing gate. Cross the Meadows tangentially via the footpath until you descend sharply to the meadow itself and the River Perry. The path continues to a rather muddy passage entrance that leads into School Lane. The red brick early twentieth century primary school is directly in front of you. Turn right and you are on Chirk Road and almost immediately back at the church where you started.

Photo: George Swift

Around Haughton, Tedsmore and Grimpo

Ron Bond

GRADE Leisurely
MAP OS Explorer™ Sheet 240
START POINT Public car park opposite Queens Head public house – Grid Ref SJ339268. Make sure you use the public car park and not the pub car park
DISTANCE 6 miles (9.66 km)
ASCENT Negligible
DURATION 3.25 hours
TERRAIN Field paths, quiet lanes and canal towpath. There may be one slightly boggy patch

A stroll round Haughton, Tedsmore and Grimpo taking in part of the Montgomery Canal.

Bordered by the railway and the canal, this is an area of Shropshire characterised by small remote villages and hamlets. It is a timeless land in which it is easy to forget the cares and troubles of the world.

The Montgomery canal, currently undergoing much restoration to re-open it after its official abandonment in 1944, runs for 38 miles from a junction with the Llangollen Canal near Ellesmere in Shropshire to Newtown in Montgomeryshire, now part of Powys. It is currently open to navigation as far as Maesbury Marsh, with plans to open a further section to Crickheath well advanced. The canal is a haven for wildlife with several Sites of Special Scientific Interest (SSI) along its length.

DIRECTIONS

1 From the car park, cross the road, go over the bridge over the canal and turn left along the road running parallel to the canal. In a few metres alongside a small building there is an access to the canal tow path. Go NE along the towpath for 1200 m and at the small building turn off right and cross the road and the take the minor road opposite towards Sutton (GR 351275).

2 Walk 700 m to a finger post on the left (just where the road begins to bear to the right). Go over the stile and immediately right (E) to a large gap in the hedge (there is a stile there also). Go through the gap and then proceed over the field to the fence alongside the railway cutting then walk along the fence to a stile to a lane. Cross the lane and go over another stile to continue in same direction alongside the railway. At the end of the field is a stile up an embankment surrounded by a badger set. Go through the gap to the right in the hedge (GR 365272).

3 Turn right (due south) and walk with the hedge on the right through four fields. There are stiles but there are gaps to walk through. Now go straight ahead through a small gate into an overgrown enclosed bridle path for short distance. Continue ahead along edge of the garden of a house named Lilac Cottage to arrive in Grimpo opposite Grimpo Cottage (GR 365264).

4 Turn left (NE) along the road signposted to Haughton. Walk along this very quiet lane for about 1 km to Haughton Church on the right (GR 372270).

5 Take the signposted path through the iron gate to the right of the church past a very small building. Follow the path through scrub for approximately 100 m (with a fence to the left) to arrive at a railway crossing. Go over the crossing (take care – trains move quickly here) and continue in the same direction (almost due south) with a hedge on the right for two fields. Then go over a stile at the side of a small disused quarry on to an enclosed path ahead and keeping the hedge on the right, through two fields. The views are now open on three sides. (Why not stop and look behind and to the left and right to enjoy the view). Continue ahead to a small wood where there is a rather well camouflaged, ancient, but solid iron stile with small steps in the right hand corner of the field-wood boundary. Go over and forward half-left. At first follow the path through beautiful woodland to a covered reservoir surrounded by iron railings. Continue ahead with the reservoir on the left, then go forward half left. (DO NOT CONTINUE STRAIGHT AHEAD). There is a waymark here and a stile at the edge of the wood will soon be visible (GR 368261).

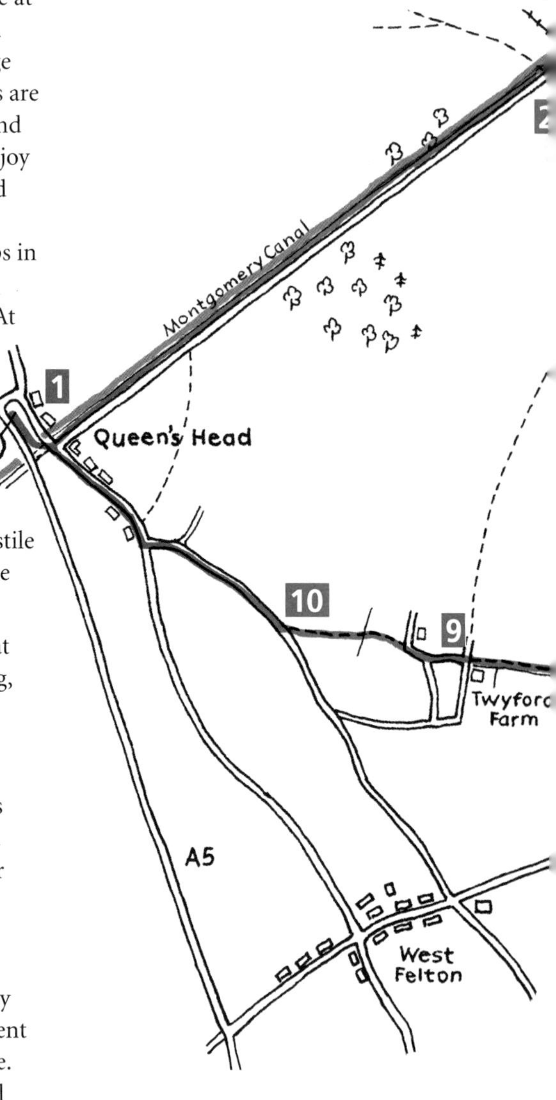

6 Go over the stile and along the field at the edge of the wood. Continue along, with a fenced track on the right, to a stile halfway along the track and on the right. Cross the stile, track and another stile to reach beautiful parkland. Walk NW across the parkland keeping well to the right of a wooded pond and to the right of a smaller hollow (these hollows sometimes contain water but can dry out). Aim for a stile approximately a third of the way from the far right hand corner of the field boundary ahead. Go over the stile and on to an ancient metal kissing gate into a tiny enclosed lane. Cross the lane and through a second small metal kissing gate opposite (GR 365261).

7 Go half right across the field to a large five barred gate on the right with a waymark. Go through the gate and across the field to a large solitary tree. From the tree head down to a fenced area near a house and walk down the left hand side with the fence on your right to a stile. Go over the stile into a bridleway (GR 362263).

8 Turn left (SW) and walk past the house to the end of the bridleway (sometimes a bit overgrown in summer). Go over a stile and across a field to a stile by the largest of three solitary trees. Cross the stile and head in the same direction well to the right of the buildings almost hidden by trees, aiming for a stile approximately ¼ of the way from the far left hand corner of the field boundary.

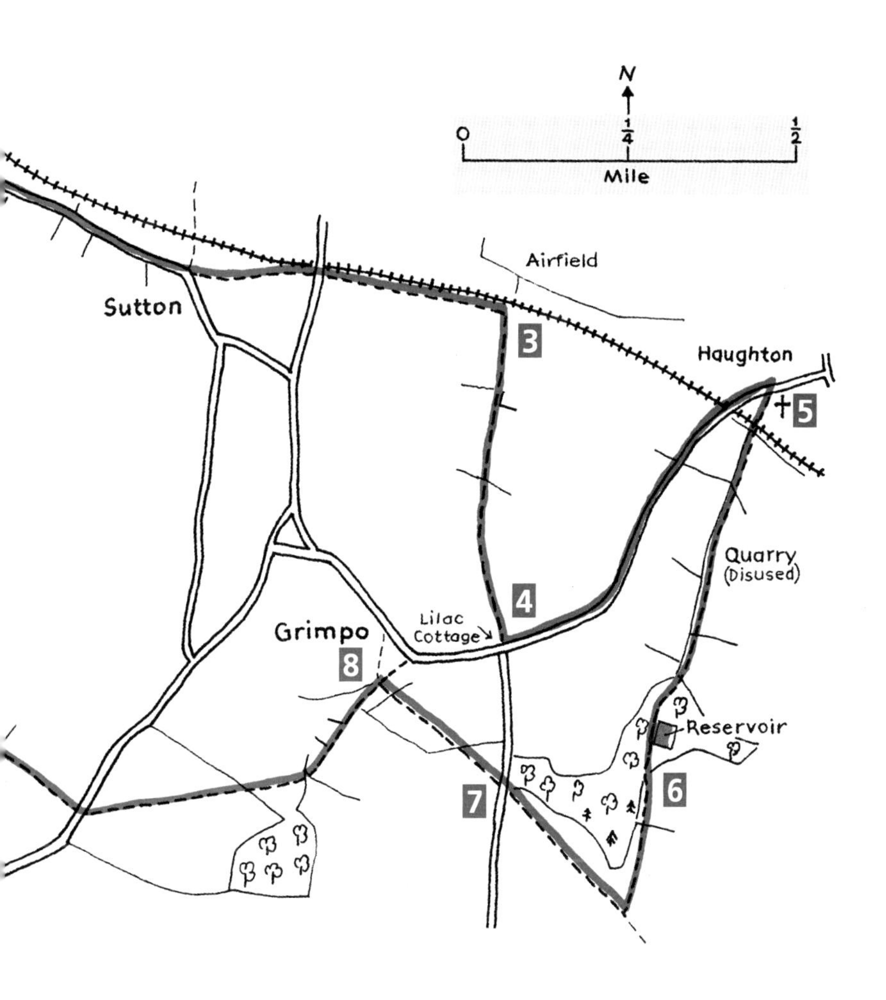

Go over the stile, cross the road into the field opposite and cross the field heading W to NW to a waymarked stile. Go over the stile and head half left over the rise and down to a stile in the field corner. Go over and left (west) along the hedge line to Twyford Farm. (Here there are many Shetland ponies and some donkeys.) (GR350263).

9 Continue to a stile in the corner and go over into a farm lane that is often messy, then left over a stile at a gate and immediately right along an enclosed farm track. At the junction go straight on and then at the white house go up a small bank to the left to find a small gate and a stile. Cross the field with the hedge on your right to a stile in the corner. Go over and half left heading for a large tree and building at a large gate (this field is often ploughed, just walk across to the gate). Go through the gate into a lane (GR 345263).

10 Turn right and then follow the lane 350 m down to a junction. Turn right and follow the road back to the Queens Head.

Nesscliffe Country Park and The Cliffe

Brian Kear

GRADE Leisurely
MAP OS Explorer™ Sheet 240
START POINT Take Hopton road out of Nesscliffe. Take first RH turn and Pine car park is signposted at top of hill – Grid Ref SJ389318
DISTANCE 5 miles (8 km)
ASCENT A series of ascents, none of which exceeds 200 ft (61 m)
DURATION 2.5 hours
TERRAIN Good paths: can be muddy in a few places and rocks can be slippery

This walk may be split into two shorter walks: Nesscliffe Hill – 2 miles (mostly woodland); The Cliffe – 3 miles (woods and heathland)

There are steep and dangerous cliffs on this walk. Keep children close to hand.

Nesscliffe Hill and Country Park covers the prominent sandstone ridge of Nesscliffe Hill and Hopton Hill and a small part of The Cliffe and is owned by Shropshire Council. The remainder of The Cliffe is common land in the parish of Ruyton XI Towns.

Nesscliffe Hill and Hopton Hill are highly wooded, which is largely coniferous. There are impressive stands of Scots pine, native oak and Redwood trees. Rhododendron has 'colonised' many areas. The Cliffe is an area of lowland heath; heather and bilberry being the main vegetation. There is a little deciduous woodland.

The area around Nesscliffe was notorious for highwaymen in the 15th and 16th century. Legend tells us that Wild Humphrey Kynaston dwelt in the cave on Nesscliffe Hill and lived the life of a Robin Hood, robbing to help the poor.

Three species of bat are known to inhabit the cave.

On the top of Nesscliffe Hill are the double ramparts of an ancient hillfort which was constructed about 2500 years ago. Archaeological finds indicate that Romans may have occupied this site in the second to the fourth century AD.

There are several quarries on Nesscliffe Hill and on The Cliffe. These were active until about 100 years ago.

There is a topograph at the highest point of The Cliffe which provides information on the surrounding hills and settlements.

DIRECTIONS

1 Leave the car park in the direction indicated by the fingerpost for Oliver's Point and Kynaston's Cave. In about 40 m turn left onto the Great Ness Road. After 60 m turn right onto a lane and go through the 5-bar gate and past a house on your right. At the junction of the paths go straight ahead. Finger-posted bridleway for Kynaston's Cave.

2 At the next fingerpost (GR 386197) fork right and follow the path signposted permissive bridleway. After 30 m turn 90 degrees right onto a footpath. You are now walking between the inner and outer ramparts of the hillfort. Part of the ramparts may still be seen here. After about 100 m turn left onto the footpath fingerposted for Oliver's Point. After about 30 m there is an information panel about Nesscliffe Hill Fort. Ramparts may be clearly seen here.

Continue in this westerly direction for 220 m to Oliver's Point which is the top of a rocky outcrop having pine trees and fallen trees. This is a good rest spot where views may be had of the Breidden hills, the River Severn and the Welsh hills (GR 386109).

(N.B. There are large, steep changes to the terrain here. Take care with children.)

3 Take the path 90 degrees left to the direction from which you came. This path goes downhill through rhododendrons and after 80 m enters a clearing with picnic tables. Follow the fingerpost for Kynaston's Cave, passing the picnic tables on your left. Shortly after leaving the clearing the footpath runs parallel with the clifftop fence. Continue with the fence on your right following signs for Kynaston's Cave. After 400 m turn right and descend the steps following the sign for Kynaston's Cave. (These steps are uneven and may be slippery). At the bottom of the steps, follow the line of the rock face on your right and after about 50 m Kynaston's Cave, where there is an information panel, will be reached (GR 383193).

4 With your back to the steps to the cave go straight ahead and after 10 m bear 45 degrees left and go down the wooden steps. At the bottom join the bridleway and turn left. Follow this bridleway through the woods. After 70 m you will pass the quarry on your left and after a further 20 m continue on the bridleway where you will have fields on your right. You will also pass an information panel about badgers. Go through the 5 bar gate at Hill Cottage and turn left up a lane (GR 389192).

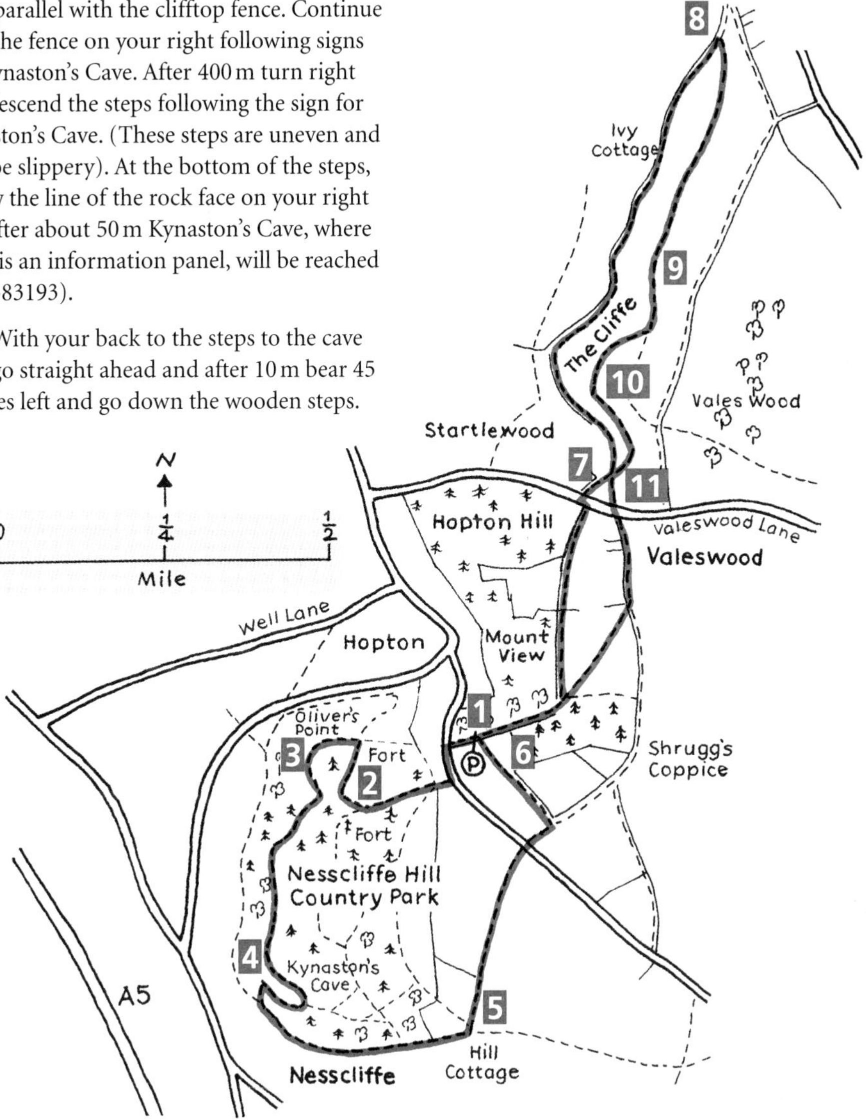

5 After 20 m bear 30 degrees right and follow the footpath through the wood with a field on your right. On leaving the wood, cross the field keeping the hedge on your right. Cross the horse gallop, cross the metalled road and go up the lane. After 60 m turn left at the signpost into a field. Proceed keeping the hedge on your right. Do not alter your direction where the hedge goes to the right. At the top of the field go through the kissing gate.

You are now back at the car park and have completed the Nesscliffe Hill section of the walk.

6 To continue the walk turn right on emerging through the kissing gate and follow the bridleway for about 450 m. (Ignore the footpath sign after 150 m and the bridleway to the right after a further 80 m).

7 At the road (Hopton to Little Ness) (GR 392323) turn left (ignore the sign for The Cliffe) and after 10 m turn right onto a footpath. After about 70 m at the T junction with a sandstone rock bridleway turn left. You will pass a small quarry on your right. Continue, with fields on your left, along this bridleway which skirts the bottom of The Cliffe. Continue straight on at the first house on your right after 600 m (GR 392308). Continue on the same path until you pass Ivy Cottage on your left. (About 25 m before Ivy Cottage you may see, on your right, the remains of two cottages which were built into the rock face.) After a further 320 m you will come to the junction of four lanes (GR 395215).

8 At this junction turn sharp right and walk up a steep incline with several houses on your left. At the top of this rise near the last house take the right fork. This will take you over the top of The Cliffe. You will pass 3 seats, the first of which is on your right and 50 m beyond the fork. After a further 150 m pass the second seat on your left and 190 m later the third seat on your left. Good views of Grinshill, the Wrekin, the Lawley, Caradoc, the Breiddens, and on a clear day, the Arran and Berwyn mountains may be seen from these points.

9 On leaving the last seat the path goes downhill and after 60 m crosses a lane and enters a wood. In the wood, 60 m after crossing the lane, take a right hand fork (which is easy to miss, so take care) which goes gently downhill for 25 m and then steeply uphill with metal railings high up on the left hand side. On leaving the wood the path gets much steeper and swings to the left. And eventually at the top of the hill you will see a topograph which identifies the surrounding hills and settlements. An excellent viewing point (GR 392206).

10 Leave this point keeping the railings of the underground reservoir on your left. Follow the path passing the information panel on your left. There is a picnic table here. The path goes downhill over some rough ground with the fence at the top of the quarry on your right. Shortly after the end of the fence the path bears right and goes steeply downhill for a short distance. On meeting the bridleway turn left and follow the bridleway for 90 m and go straight across the Little Ness to Hopton Road at Valeswood (GR 393203).

11 After 160 m follow the footpath sign into the wood, ignoring the bridleway. After 140 m bear right at the fingerpost in the wood and after a further 90 m turn left onto the bridleway. A further 150 m and you will be back at the car park.

Note You may have noticed the many footpaths and bridleways branching from this walk which could provide many more pleasant hours of discovery in this area.

Kinnerley

Dave Arden

Grade	Leisurely
Map	OS Explorer™ Sheet 240
Start point	St Mary's Church – Grid Ref SJ338209. Parking is available by the Village Green or at the nearby Village Hall.
Public Transport	On Bus Route 576 from Oswestry to Shrewsbury
Distance	4 miles (6.45 km)
Ascent	Negligible
Duration	Approximately 2.5 hours
Terrain	Good tracks and paths, some fields and a number of stiles

A scenic walk around Kinnerley taking in the village of Dovaston.

Kinnerley is mentioned in the Domesday Book and in the 13th century the castle was occupied no less than three times by the Welsh Prince Llewellyn. The site of the castle was almost certainly the mound at Belan, with the castle being a motte and bailey defensive structure.

Today Kinnerley is a pleasant village situated more than a mile from the two nearest main roads, the B4396 and the A5. However, a network of lanes links it with various small hamlets and the main roads. The centre of the village is the village green which is surrounded by St Mary's Church, the village shop and Post Office and the Cross Keys public house. The church is built of local red sandstone and the west tower dates back to the 1600s; the village shop, built of yellow 'Oswestry' brick, was originally a combined shop, bakery and farm.

Directions

1 From St Mary's Church, take the lane by the side of the Church wall and follow the track until a tarmac lane is reached. Turn left and follow the lane round to a track leading up to a field (GR 341208).

2 At the stile, go diagonally across the field to the right and cross the following field to reach a tarmac lane (called Gully Lane) (GR 345207).

3 Turn left, and at the kennels take the right fork. At the T-junction go straight ahead into the field and continue up past the Church (GR 349212).

4 Turn right and go along the road for a short distance and then go over the stile on the left. In the second field bear left across to a small group of trees, go over a stile and keeping to the hedge cross to another stile, then go diagonally across the next field to the far right hand corner (GR 349216).

5 Turn left and follow the track round until a stile on the right is reached. Cross the stile and follow the path across three fields to reach a small footbridge in the far right hand corner of the third field (GR 349217).

6 After the bridge turn left and after crossing the next stile keep to the left hand side of a large field to locate a stile near the centre of the hedge in front. Head right across the next field towards a gate to a lodge (GR 343221).

At this point if refreshment is required it is possible to continue out to the road, turn left and walk into the village of Knockin to the Bradford Arms or the village shop.

7 From the gate by the lodge head back towards Kinnerley, straight across the field following the bridleway signs; by a small copse follow the hedge round to the left to meet a track (GR 345216).

8 Turn right onto this track and on reaching the road turn left and then shortly right (GR 345213).

9 Continue along the lane and then take the next lane right which will come back to the kennels (step 3) and then return to the start on the original outward route.

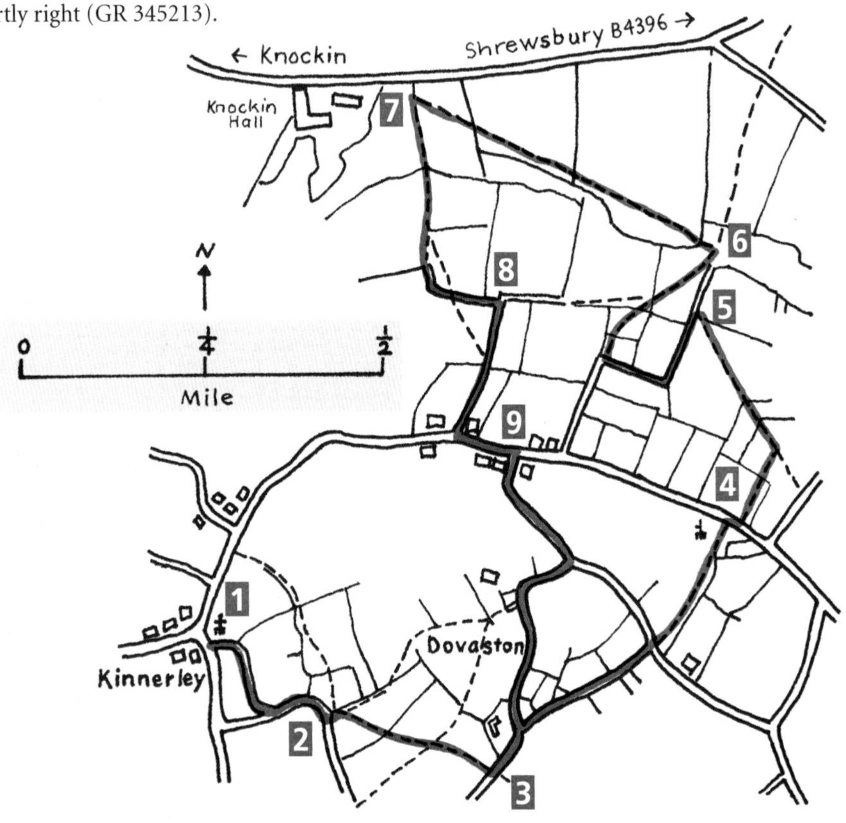

Rodney's Pillar

Graham Dean

GRADE Moderate
MAP OS Explorer™ Sheet 240
START POINT Car park near village of Criggion – Grid Ref SJ294148
DISTANCE 4 miles (6.45 km)
ASCENT Approximately 975 ft (300 m)
DURATION 2-3 hours
TERRAIN Good paths, but one short, steep descent that can be avoided

This walk utilises permissive footpaths that are closed every Tuesday from 25 October to 1 February.

A short hill walk that provides panoramic views over Shropshire and Mid Wales.

The Pillar is visible for many miles and can be seen long before entering the area. Built in 1781 in honour of Admiral Sir George Brydges Rodney, the pillar was officially 'opened' on 10 August 1782. The original Welsh inscription on the pillar read 'The highest pillars will fall, The strongest towers will decay, But the fame of Sir George Brydges Rodney shall increase continually, And his good name shall never be obliterated'.

Rodney was born in 1718 and died in 1792 although it is not believed he ever visited the area or had anything to do with the erection of the pillar. It is said the pillar was built on Breidden because oak from the area was sold to build Admiral Rodney's ships and the local landowners wanted to honour him. Originally the pillar was topped with a 'golden' ball, which was destroyed in 1835 by lightning. A new copper ball was installed in 1847 when the original sustained further damage. The last repairs took place in 1967.

This walk is the easiest way up and down the Breidden Hill, but an Ordnance Survey map will reveal that the area is crisscrossed with paths and permissive forest trails.

Fallow deer are commonly seen and woodland birds are abundant in the broadleaf and conifer forest. Whitethroats inhabit the scrub, stonechats the bracken and ravens, buzzards, peregrines, skylarks and meadow pipits can be seen.

Before the walk, why not visit St Michael's Church, Criggion. Its churchyard is surrounded by an unusual dry moat (a flood defence). After the walk, the Admiral Rodney Pub, just up the road, provides welcome refreshment.

DIRECTIONS

1 Go through the car park gate next to an information board and turn left to go up a forestry road for about 30 to 40 minutes.

2 At a fork in the road (GR 303143) you will find a log bench with weird squirrels chainsaw-carved into it. Take the right hand fork and continue for 20 to 25 minutes along a flat track through the woods until you come to a pond where benches and a picnic table are located (GR 296139).

3 From the pond take the right hand fork and almost immediately turn right through a waymarked gate. Follow the path until you go through a gap in the fence and see a waymarker post directly ahead (GR295142).

4 From the waymarker post continue straight on up the bridleway that curves up and around to the top of Breiddon Hill passing a topograph that provides information on all the surrounding hills and settlements.

5 The triangulation pillar (GR 295144) (365 m) marks the top of the Breidden Hill and should have been reached in about 1.25 to 1.5 hours. Rodney's Pillar itself provides a good place to have some refreshments and view the wiggly oxbow bends of the river Severn below.

Descend on a steep path beyond Rodney's Pillar, bearing right after the white triangulation pillar that is indicated by a way marker post part way down the path. *

6 At a stile (GR 297143) go over the stile and in a short distance go through a gate and walk on until a waymarker post is reached (GR 303144).

7 At the waymarker post turn right and soon you will intersect the forest road you ascended. Turn left to return to the start.

* To avoid this steep decent you can retrace your steps back to the way marker post in step 4, turn left and follow the fence to the stile at the start of step 6.

8 The points marked 8 on the sketch map are alternative ways up and down but are very steep, wet and muddy.

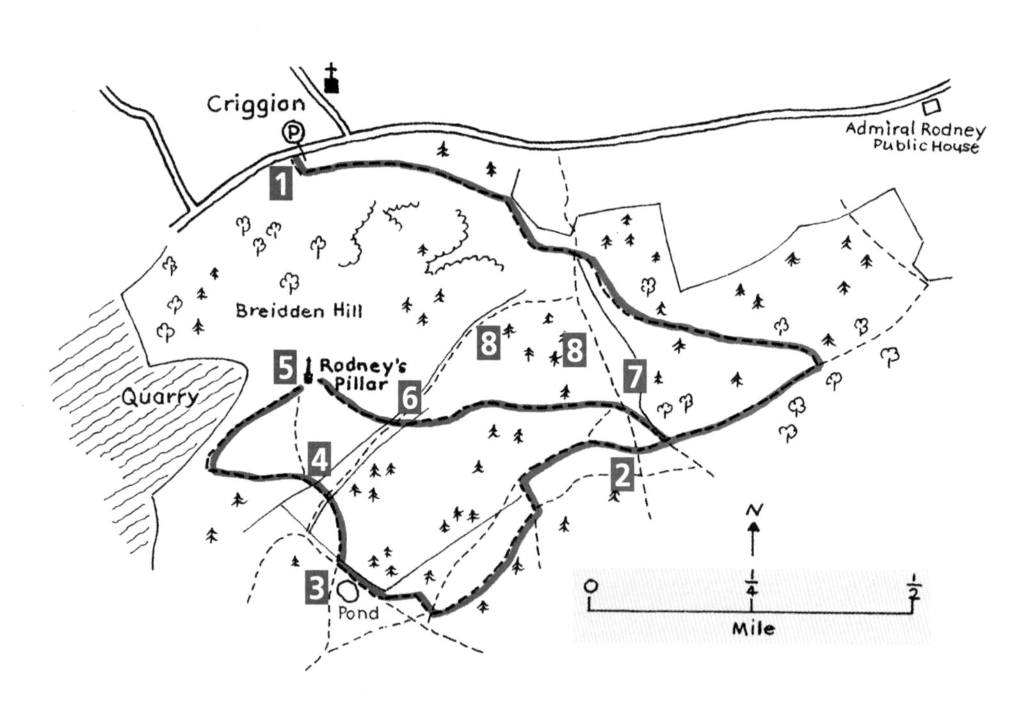

Llanymynech Heritage Site, Llanymynech Hill and the Montgomery Canal

Sally Barrett

Grade	Moderate
Map	OS Explorer™ Sheet 240
Start point	Public car park beside the Dolphin public house (going south, turn right off the A483 in Llanymynech onto the B4398 and then after approx 50 m, right again into the car park) – Grid Ref SJ266209
Distance	3.9 miles (6.28 km)
Ascent	Approximately 1050 ft (320 m)
Duration	2.5 hours
Terrain	Good paths and tracks

A varied walk through the Heritage Area then up onto the hill, across the golf course, back along the escarpment with its stunning views, and finally along the Montgomery Canal. A shorter (and less steep) walk can be taken by leaving out the golf course and Llanymynech Hill.

Although this walk is barely 4 miles, allow plenty of time to view the Hoffman Kiln and other relics from the lime works.

Llanymynech has been an important settlement since a hillfort was established in the 10th Century BC. Offa's Dyke passes through the village and mining in the area dates back to Roman times. Most of the industrial remains today are from 19th and 20th century limeworks. Much of the local rock outcrop on the hill above the village is the result of quarrying over the centuries. Canal and later rail transport, allowed limestone quarrying and burning – to produce quicklime – to expand rapidly. The main uses of Llanymynech limestone were in agriculture, building, iron and steel.

Portland cement spelled the end for the lime industry. A brave, final bid for survival was the construction of the Hoffman Kiln in 1898, which ran until 1914. This was really a series of individual kilns arranged around a tunnel, enabling the non-stop production of quicklime.

Rich hay meadows surround the Hoffman site, and the woodland on the same site has an abundance of wild spring flowers. A good selection of alkaline preferring plants and interesting ferns grow near the kiln, and many different orchids can be seen on the quarry site. There is a pair of peregrine falcons on the quarry site. At least 34 species of bird can be found on the heritage site including buzzards, finches, goldcrests, nuthatches, warbler and woodpeckers.

Directions

1 At the rear of the car park, go through the gate and turn right onto the towpath. Go under the road bridge then immediately right up the steps, turn right at the top and into the small heritage car park (if there is space, this is an alternative car parking place). Walk into the heritage site along the lane from the heritage car park. Note the disused Cambrian Railway line on your left above you. You pass a sunken tramway on your left which leads to the Middleton dock on the right. You may also notice a raised embankment in the trees running towards the canal and another larger dock on the right. Turn left (note the sign 'Llanymynech Limeworks Heritage Area') towards the old stable block. This is now an educational centre with a mini kiln on the end of the building. Turn right at the junction and walk past a red brick floor with engine/compressor fittings to two draw kilns, built by Thomas Savin in 1871. Follow the wall to the stone steps just before the chimney (GR 268212).

2 Go up the steps to the magnificent Hoffman Kiln and Chimney.

The Hoffman Kiln, with its flue systems and cloister-like arches, is really worth exploring. Limestone was burned to produce lime in a continuous process; a section was packed with limestone, with a narrow wall of coal fed from the top. While this burned the next section was worked on, the coal catching fire from the heat in the previous section, and so on for 14 sections. The result was a much more efficient use of fuel than the old lime kilns, but the working conditions were terrible.

Continue along the track up past the Hoffman with the big embankment on the left, and carry on for approximately 50 m. Turn left at the stream and go through to the main path. Turn right and continue to the ruined red house which was the Tally house (GR 267215).

3 Continue bearing left under the A483. This is the start of the 1 in 4 inclined plane, known as the Bridgeman incline after the family who owned part of the hill and later had the title Earl of Bradford. Follow this, now a much rougher path, up the hill, through a metal kissing gate and continue up to the English winding drum house (GR 267216), with its fitted replica self acting braked winch drum. The weight of the loaded trucks descending by the force of gravity was counterbalanced by them pulling the empty trucks up, although a brake was applied to stop them going too fast (There is also a restored 25 ft high draw kiln close by.)

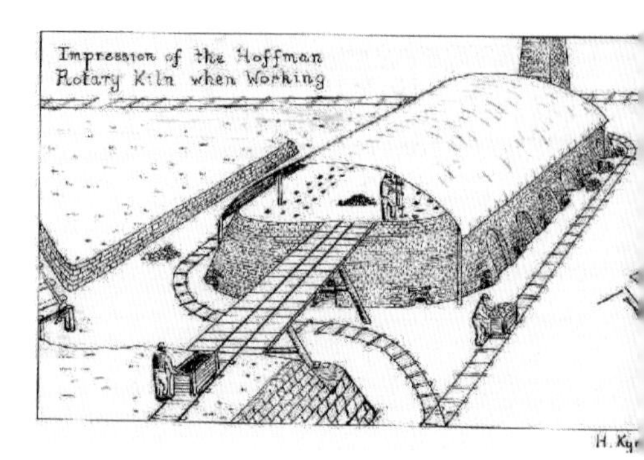

4 Turn right at the English winding drum onto a wide metalled track below the quarry wall. Further along there could be climbing activity. Keep a look out here for the protective fencing on the right surrounding the top of four draw kilns. Just before a metal gate and kissing gate, turn left, cross the stream and then left again following the stone wall and wrought iron fence on your right for a few metres. Turn right at the end of the wall and go up the hill along a narrow path which starts to climb again (beyond the metal gate is the Nature Reserve car park and the start of the shorter route) (GR 271219).

5 Go through a metal kissing gate, climb to a stile by a cottage, continue up, across another stile and join a track (bearing

Interior of the Hoffman Kiln

right). The track continues uphill and meets a tarmac lane at Holly Bank (GR 270221).

6 Turn left onto the lane and continue to its end. At the entrance to the golf club, follow the fingerpost for the bridal way across the green towards a single tree on the horizon. The bridleway is well marked across the golf course by a series of small wooden guide posts. You should pass to the right of Llanymynech clubhouse, across a second stretch of grass and past a fairway (on your left) up to a gritted track where there is a small hut. Follow this track to reach the tree first seen on the horizon, a silver birch (GR 264221).

7 Continue over the summit (admiring the views of the Berwyn hills and Tanat valley), and follow the way marks to the edge of the golf course, where the bridleway meets Offa's Dyke Path (GR 261219).

8 Turn left onto Offa's Dyke Path through a wooden gate. The path descends slowly through woods and enters open heath land (GR 261217), which covers the old quarry workings and spoil heaps, giving panoramic views, with the Lime Kiln Chimney and Llanymynech spread out in the near distance.

Follow the Offa's Dyke Path marks carefully, passing the entrance to the quarry on your left (GR 264216).

9 Continue ahead passing the Welsh Winding House and inclined plane on the right until you reach a wooden kissing gate onto the upper path (GR 265216).

10 The Offa's Dyke Path turns off right, but continue on the current path to the English Winding House. You now repeat part of the path already covered, continuing to the Nature Reserve car park (GR271219 – see step 4) but this time go through the metal gate and kissing gate until the track becomes a road. Continue on this road to the A483 (GR 272218).

11 Cross the A483 and before walking down Rhiew Revel Lane, make a small diversion to the left to Gyn Lane and the gin wheel (GR 272218), which used to haul the trams up from the canal.

Return and continue down Rhiew Revel Lane and just before the Montgomery Canal bridge, notice the six old lime kilns on the left (GR 274218).

12 Cross the bridge and join the towpath by turning left and going under the bridge. The canal is dry here but the intention is to make it navigable in the future. Follow the towpath, past one of the restored black and white metal mile posts which seem to point to Newtown 25 miles/Welsh Frankton 10 miles in the wrong direction, until you realise the sign is curved, to tell the barges where they are going to rather than where they have come from. Continue past a quay at the old Cambrian Railway bridge, to the start of the navigable section of canal. Here a path branches right along the edge of the field towards the Lime Kiln Chimney, but we continue on the left bank of the canal towards the Heritage Centre, passing the George Watson Buck moored at the Centre and then return to the car park via the gate from the towpath.

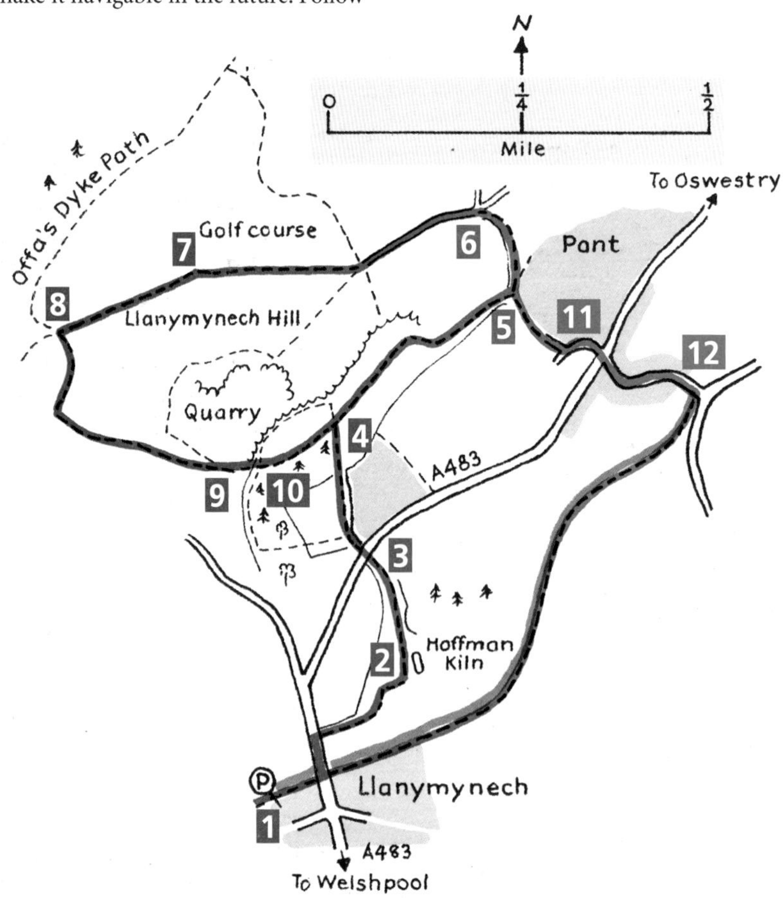

Penybontfawr Hill and forest circuit walks

Ron Bond

Two walks are described here which can be combined to provide a 9.5 mile circuit

Grade	Strenuous
Map	OS Explorer™ Sheet 239
Start point	Free car park in Penybontfawr – Grid Ref SJ 088245
Distance	Walk 1: 4.8 miles (7.7 km) Walk 2: 6 miles (9.7 km) Walk 3: 9.5 miles (15.3 km)
Ascent	Walk 1: 820 ft (250 m) Walk 2: 1000 ft (305 m) Walk 3: 2000 ft (610 m)
Duration	Walk 1: 2.5 hours Walk 2: 3 hours Walk 3: 5 hours
Terrain	Paths, lanes, fields and woods. There are steep ascents and descents

The walk reveals views in all directions that cannot be had from the valley bottom. There is a pub at the start and there is the Plough Inn at Llanrhaeadr two miles down the road that serves a full selection of food.

Penybontfawr (formerly known as Bont Fawr) sits in the narrow Tanat Valley alongside the River Tanat. The settlement is almost all 19th century in origin and owes its existence to its strategic position on the crossroads of the toll roads between west Wales, Bala to the north, Oswestry to the east and Shrewsbury to the southeast.

The Tanat Light Railway which operated from 1904 until its progressive closure during the 1950s and 60s passed through Penybontfawr with the station located alongside the river just to the north of the village. The station site is now a small modern housing development. The only reminder of the railway now is the Railway Inn in the village. The railway's principle purpose here was to serve the mines and quarries further up the Tanat Valley at Llangynog. A visit to Llangynog will reveal the mining and quarrying past, in the shape of the spoil tips, ruined mine buildings, tramways and inclines.

The area of the walk, to the west of Penybontfawr, is characterised today as being mainly sheep farming country with steep hills and moorland. There is an abundance of bird life with almost constantly circling buzzards much in evidence.

Directions

Walk 1

1 Head WNW along the main road and in 250 m go over the bridge and fork left (signposted Llanwyddn). Walk along the road for 400 m then turn right past a cottage named Pentre Isaf on the left. In 200 m, at a T-junction, turn left and walk along the lane for 1 km, then turn right through a gateway into a farm with no obvious name but marked Bache-doethion on the map. There is a large corrugated iron barn near the road (GR 073242).

2 Go up the steep concrete drive to the farmhouse, past the buildings on left. Leaving the farmhouse on the right go through a metal gate and up steeply on a rough track. In 150 m go through a metal gate and immediately right at the T-junction just below a small wood. Follow the track round and head almost north on a bearing of 340°, then go through an ancient gateway between walls (no gate at time of writing). Stay on the track through two gates close together, *Do not go left along the tempting green lane alongside the wall.* Continue west on track over the shoulder of the hill and through a series of metal gates, staying on a stony track that becomes grassy and then leads into a field. Continue ahead bearing left (SW) to the far corner of the wood (GR 055248). At this point there is a fine view of the two valleys to the north. Note: In case of difficulty it is possible at this point to follow the track down to Llangynog.

3 Go left through the iron gate, along the path on the NW side of the wood to a wooden gate on the right. *Do not go through the gate* but turn left almost due south down into the forest. Follow blue bridleway signs along the edge of the forest on a clear path (views down the valley at this point) and go past the spoil heaps on the right. At a junction with a forest track, where the way ahead divides, go left (south) onto a double track bridleway and through a ford at 300 m. Then continue on the track for a further 600 m to a path on the left (Note: this path is difficult to see – it initially turns back on the bridleway). Look for a way marker sign and at this point, turn right to follow a stone wall down to a wooden gate. Go through the gate and bear diagonally down a small field into an enclosed sunken lane. Follow the lane down to a road, passing a farmhouse and buildings (Cwmwr-Isaf) on the left (GR 064238).

4 Turn left and walk for 750 m along the road ignoring the turning at point 5. Opposite the farm Ty-nant, turn left along a minor lane and in 300 m the entrance to Bache-doethion will be passed on the left. Continue down the lane for about 1 km and turn right down a small lane. At the T-junction turn left into Penybontfawr to return to the car park.

Walk 2

1 Head WNW along the main road and in 250 m go over the bridge and fork left (signposted Llanwyddn). Walk along the road for 400 m then turn right past a cottage named Pentre Isaf on the left. In 200 m, at a T junction, turn left and walk along the lane for 1 km to a farm with no obvious name but marked Bache-doethion on the map. There is a large corrugated iron barn near the road (GR 073242).

2 Continue straight along the lane for 800 m, ignoring the first lane on the left, to arrive at a second small lane on the left (GR 067238).

5 Take the lane that goes left, leaving a large cottage on the left and continue right, crossing a bridge over Afon Hirnant. Continue uphill on the road for 150 m then turn right through a gate with a bridleway sign on a post. Follow the obvious bridleway SW up through one large gate and four small bridleway gates to a small enclosed green-lane. Follow the lane to a T-junction and then turn left and head to the road (GR 059226).

6 Cross the road and take the bridleway opposite to continue south. Follow the track up to the edge of the forest and go through an iron gate then continue forward for 150 m. Turn left at a small post with a bridleway sign and follow the path south alongside forest for 350 m to cross a slippery bridge (GR 060217).

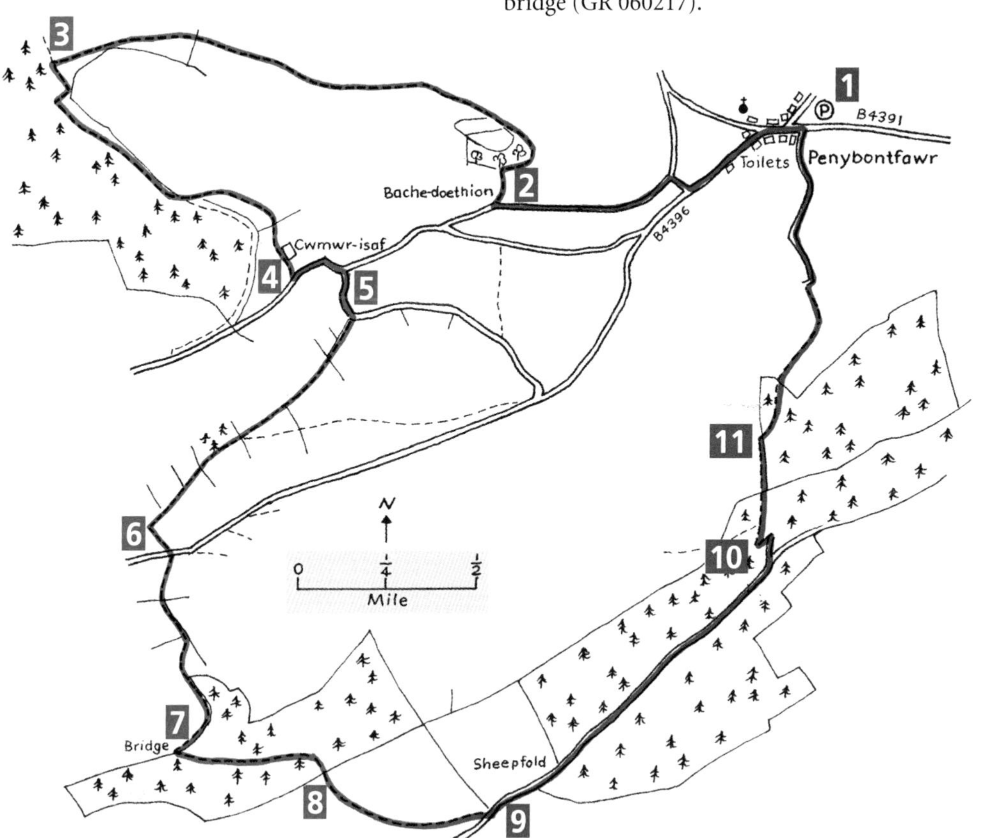

7 Go through the bridleway gate and follow the path left (east) through the forest. In 750 m the path swings south then in another 200 m go through a bridleway gate into a field (GR 067216).

8 Continue ahead with the fence on the right and when the fence dips away downhill follow the contour east on a small path to reach a metalled track (GR 0742214).

9 Turn left along the track passing a large sheepfold on the right. Go through a gate and continue along the track NE through the forest. (The surface of the track deteriorates but is still metalled). There are dazzling views to the right (SE). *Ignore tracks to right and left* and in 1.3 km, at a large circular clearing, take the signposted bridleway on the left (GR087226).

10 Climb steeply up heading north on a narrow path leaving wide but low metal gates behind. At the forest track that crosses the hill go left and then quickly right (north) up a rough but clear and obvious track. At the top go through a gate into a field and then steeply downhill for 350 m with a forest fence on the right. Turn right through a bridleway gate in the fence (GR 086231).

11 In 20 m go left at the signpost and head very steeply downhill on an obvious path through the trees. At the end of the forest enter a field over a stile and continue downhill NE then north along a line of trees on an obvious sunken track. Go through a gate at the bottom of the field and take a track on the right leaving a farm on the left. Continue down the track that soon becomes a metalled road, passing a farmhouse on the left and follow the lane down to Penybontfawr to return to the start of the walk.

Walk 3

This is essentially walks 1 and 2 combined without the return to Penybontfawr in the middle.

Start with Walk 1, Steps 1 to the end of Step 3. Continue from point 4 on the map down the lane to the first turning on the right (point 5 on the map). Continue with Walk 2 from Step 5 to the end.

Photo: Peter Carr

The Moelydd

Helen Hunter-Hayes

Grade	Moderate
Map	OS Explorer™ Sheet 240
Start point	Chapel Green car park (opposite the church in Trefonen) – Grid Ref SJ260267
Distance	4.3 miles (7.3 km)
Ascent	Approximately 325 ft (100 m)
Duration	2.5 hours
Terrain	Good paths and tracks

A scenic walk to the top of the Moelydd. Provides panoramic views of the surrounding area.

The Moelydd was once the site of lead workings – perhaps in the 17th century. Numerous pits and craters can be seen, that follow the line of the mineral ore.

At the top of the Moelydd is a memorial inscription to Dumville Lees who was killed in the first world war. His father, John Dumville Lees, lived at Woodville and was a benefactor of the Trefonen and Treflach area.

Directions

1 Leave the car park and pass the Barley Mow and turn right into Bellan Lane, past the village shop/Post Office on the left, until the lane bends to the right. At this point leave Bellan Lane and carry on straight ahead along a track, over a stile and into a field (GR 257266).

2 You are now on the Offa's Dyke Path (marked with the sign of an acorn). Go straight on with the hedge on your right and cross another stile. Bear slightly left and go over the stone slab bridge over Trefonen Brook (it may be muddy), and then over the next stile. Continue to follow the Offa's Dyke Path straight ahead, going uphill with an old hollow way on your left. You will pass two large trees, one of which is a small leaved lime, which is indigenous to the Welsh border area. Continue to the next stile and cross into a lane (GR 250262).

3 Still following Offa's Dyke Path, leaving the stile, turn left and then almost immediately right to Canol farm and continue on through the farmyard and through the gate along the track. Take the stile on the right and continue up hill with the hedge on your right. At the marker post, turn left and follow the track up to the stile, cross it and turn right. Continue to follow the Offa's Dyke signs to the top of The Moelydd (GR245253).

4 From the top of The Moelydd continue down the track keeping to the Offa's Dyke Path until you reach the road. Ignore the footpath off to the left into Jones Rough (GR 248247).

5 Cross the stile into a lane and turn left. Follow the lane round past the entrance to the disused Nantmawr quarry (along this lane the Offa's Dyke Path will leave your route going off to the right).

6 Now take the track on the left past the old engine house and up to a gate with steps and a stile on the right. Go over the stile and, keeping the buildings on your left, continue to a gate. Go through the gate and follow the track down for about 90 m, then go over a slight rise and bear slightly right through a coppice to a stile onto a small lane (GR 256252).

7 Turn left and go along the lane to a stile on the left near Red House farm. Cross the stile and keeping the farm and fence on the right, continue uphill to the next stile. Continue on to a stile with buildings on the right and take the gate into the field, go straight ahead to a stile into a lane. Ignore the stile directly in front of you (although this is a more direct route this field is invariably boggy even in the driest of weather), turn left and continue up the lane which takes you back to point 3 (GR 250262). Continue down the field over the stile and retrace your steps back into the village.

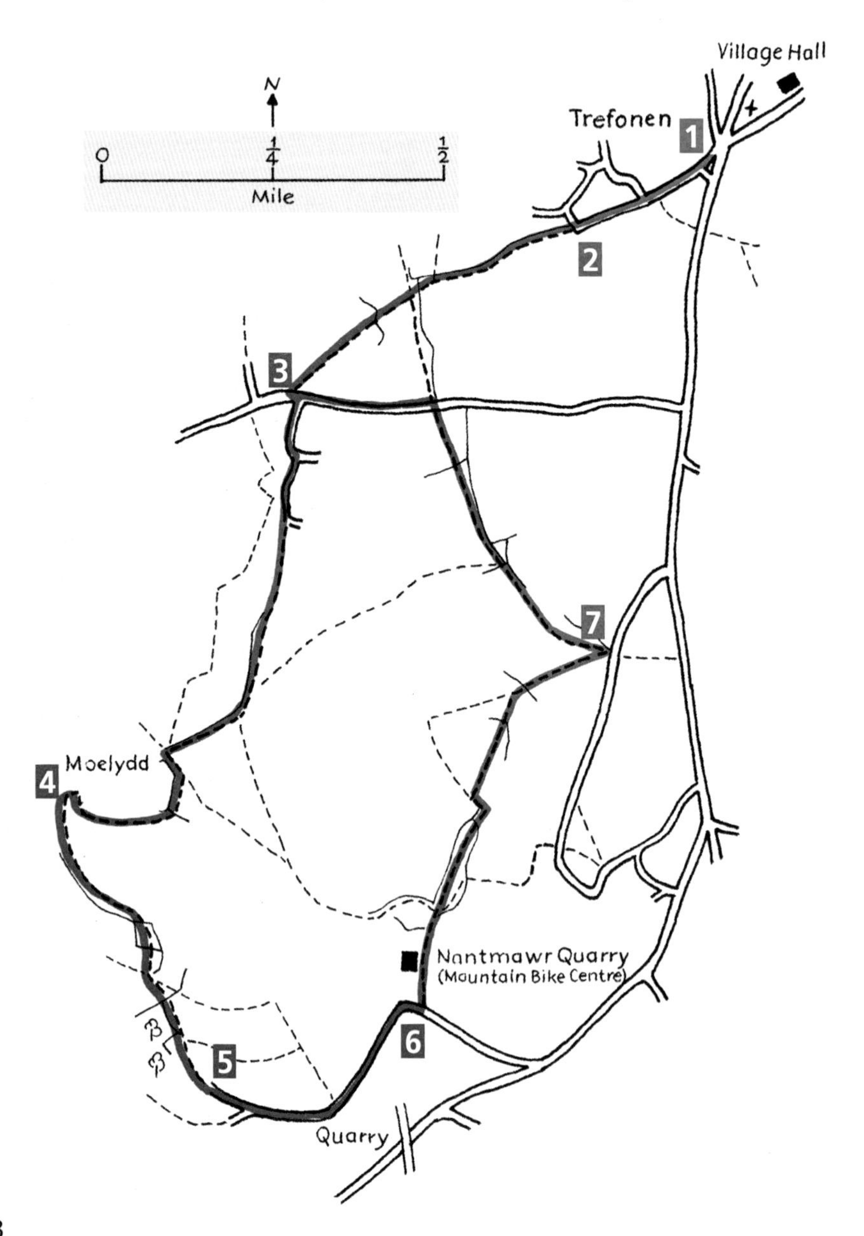

Walk through Weston to Morda and back

Ron Bond

Grade Leisurely
Map OS Explorer™ Sheet 240
Start point Queens Road, Oswestry Grid Ref SJ291291
Distance 5.6 miles (9.0 km)
Ascent Approximately 100 ft (30 m)
Duration 3 hours
Terrain Paths, lanes and fields. Some very easy ascent and no difficult descent

This walk starts in Oswestry, passes the town cemetery, Weston Mill and continues through a pastoral area that was once a centre for brick making and mining, before returning to Oswestry.

Mining started around Morda in the late 18th/early 19th century and consisted of simple bell pits. The remains can be identified as depressions in the fields. Later, mining developed into a full sized colliery when the Drill colliery (also known as the Gronwen Colliery) opened in 1836. This was the only mine in the area that accessed all seven coal seams running beneath Morda. The much larger output than the bell pits led to the development of a tramway from the colliery to Gronwen Bridge on the Montgomery Canal to aid the speedy distribution of the coal. In 1842 the Sweeney Colliery was started. However, its short life was plagued by flooding and it was soon abandoned. The Sweeny Brickworks operated on a site nearby, with clay extracted from deposits above the coal seam. The brickworks produced both red and blue bricks, pipes and tiles.

From the late 18th and throughout the 19th century the Morda stream provided power to drive machinery for a number of factories within the Morda Valley. These included a print works, woollen mills and corn mills. The mill at Penyllan is perhaps the best preserved and was used to grind corn. The chimney and boiler house were added in the 1860s. However, these were never used.

Directions

1 Take the enclosed footpath opposite No 8 in Queens Road and walk 100 m to the end then go through the kissing gate into the field. Turn right and walk along the edge, 150 m, to the end of the field. Turn left and follow the path between the hedge and the cemetery fence (this path can be muddy and slippery in wet weather). At the end, go right through the kissing gate and across the field to next gate. Through the gate and half left down to and through another kissing gate, then along an enclosed path to a T-junction of paths. Turn right in an enclosed path and follow 400 m to a further kissing gate onto Weston Lane (GR 294282).

2 Turn left and proceed for 400 m to the T-junction at Weston Mill. Turn right along Weston Road for 150 m, round the bend and over a bridge and then take the footpath over the marked stile on the left (GR 295276).

3 In 25 m turn right over a stile and walk across the field diagonally to, and over, a stile in the corner near a large oak tree. Turn right onto a track and take the nearby stile on the left and continue diagonally in the same SW direction. Cross stiles to the corner of the wood on the left, which has a large lake inside. Go round the edge of the wood and across the field again heading SW and then go over a stile to the B5069 (GR 289271).

4 Taking care, cross the B5069 and walk up the road opposite, go round the left hand bend, passing the end of a house drive, to a marked enclosed footpath on the right. Take the path up to the stile and go over into the field. Keeping the hedge on the right, walk across the field to the fence and then turn left (SW) along the fence to a stile. Don't cross the stile, but pass it by and walk diagonally half left part way down the bank and over the fence stile. Passing the back of a house on the left, go down to a stile in the corner of the field, then over and out into a lane. Turn right up the lane. In 100 m (past some houses) go over the stile up the bank on the right. Cross the field due north, go over another stile and across the next field in the same direction to a road (GR 281271).

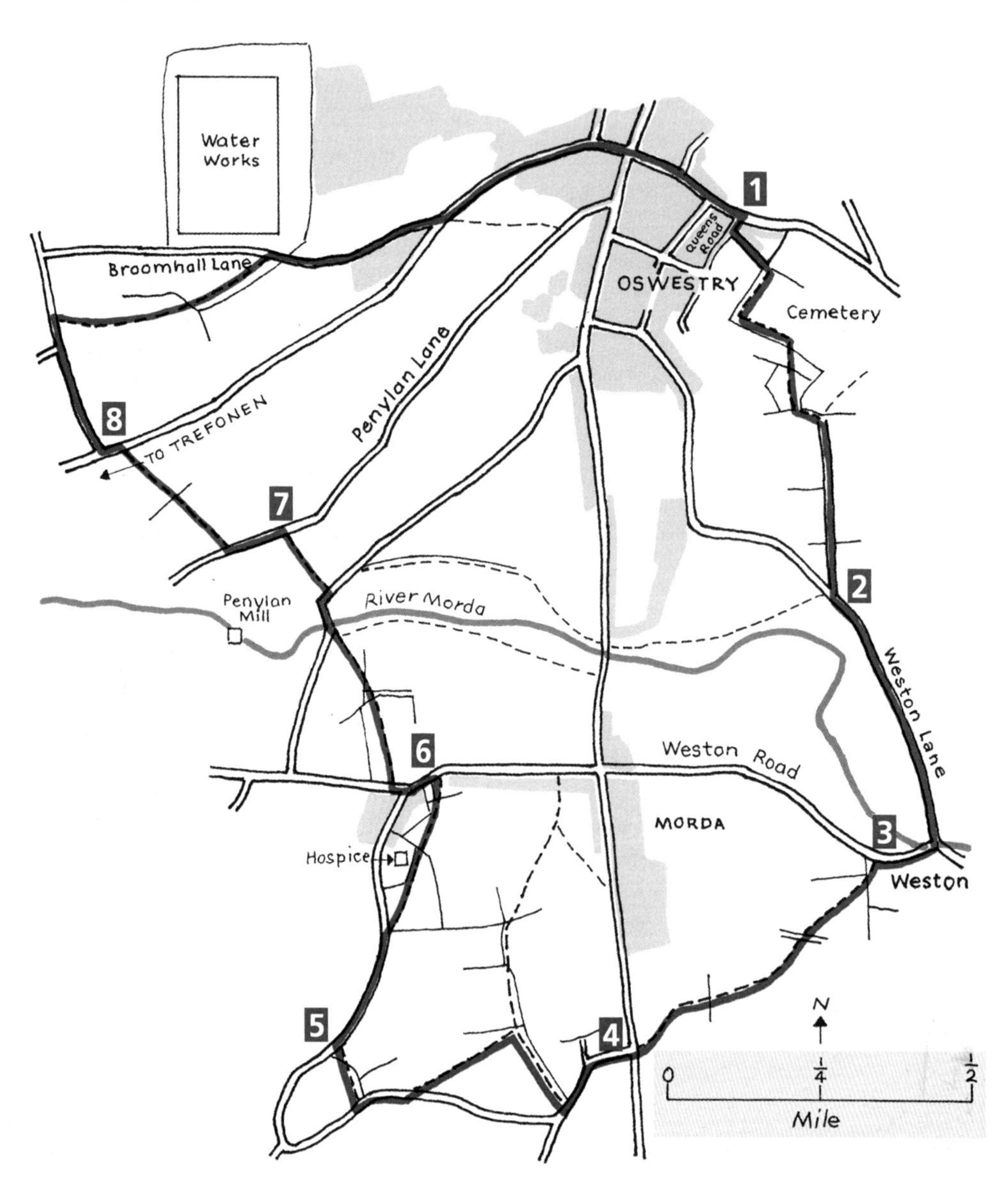

5 Turn right along the road, past a large farmhouse that was once the mine HQ, and in 350 m take the signed footpath over a stile by a large gate on the right. Go across the field due north to a stile, then cross over into the grounds of the Children's Hospice (Hope House) on the left. Follow a very clear path down and then past a pond over a stile into a field. Turn left along the hedge to arrive at a stile into the driveway of Llwyn Mapsis. Go over the stile and out on to the road (GR 284278).

6 Turn left uphill slightly and in 100 m take the footpath over the stile on the right. (The OS map is slightly wrong here and shows the path away from the hedge whereas the agreed line is along the hedge row.) With the hedge on the left cross the field to a stile, go over and down a stepped bank (these steps can be very slippery when wet). Penylan Mill with its tall chimney is in the valley ahead. Now head down the field diagonally to the right, just west of north, to arrive at a stile near Morda brook. Go over the stile, turn right over the bridge and head along Croeswyllan Lane 50 m to a stile in front. Go over it and then head up the hill past a telephone pole to a stile into Penylan Lane (GR 280283).

7 Turn left along Penylan Lane and in 120 m, just past the drive to some cottages, take the path over a stile up a slight bank on the right. Cross the field (NW) to a stile in the hedge, go over and continue NW to the Oswestry/Trefonen road (GR 275285).

8 Taking care, cross this fast busy road onto the pavement opposite, go left for 20 m and then turn right on to a minor road. In 350 m, at a footpath crossing, turn right and cross a field bearing left from a track to a stile in the left hand corner. Go over the stile and heading in the same direction go to the far field corner and over a stile near an electricity supply pylon and a house into Broomhall Lane. Turn right down Broomhall Lane to Trefonen Road, then left down past the school for 500 m to the traffic lights. Cross the road and go straight on to the third turning on right which is Queens Road.

Photo: Peter Carr

Racecourse to Pant Glas

Peter & Audrey Ibbotson

Grade	Moderate
Map	OS Explorer™ Sheet 240
Start point	Car park at Oswestry Old Racecourse – Grid Ref SJ259305
Distance	5 miles (8 km)
Ascent	Approximately 750 ft (230 m)
Duration	2.5 hours
Terrain	Field paths and quiet lanes with some short steep hill climbs and one long steady climb along a road. The walk can be quite muddy in places, especially after heavy rain

This walk offers good views over Oswestry and the countryside beyond to the distant hills, including Rodney's Pillar on Breidden Hill (see Rodney's Pillar walk) and the Wrekin. This walk can be put together with the next walk to make an approximate 8.5 mile walk.

Oswestry Old Racecourse was the site of horse racing on common land from the mid-18th century for about 100 years. It was a figure of eight course, crossing on the top of Mount Road hill. It fell into decline with the advent of the railways offering better transport for horses, riders and spectators to other courses. Stone ruins of the Grandstand remain where Offa's Dyke Path crosses the Racecourse, and there is a more recent horse monument nearby (see also Racecourse and Candy Woods walk).

Pant Glas village (which translates as 'green valley') was originally built to house workers on the Brogyntyn Estate owned by Lord Harlech. It included a school which is now a private residence.

Directions

Caution: Care is needed crossing Mount Road as traffic travels very quickly down this moderately steep hill.

1 Leave the car park by the way you entered, onto the road and turn left. In about 50 m take the first stile on the right. Follow the left hand hedge downhill, past the balcony (LHS), for about 200 m to the post waymark. Turn right to the field corner and go over the stile. Continue downhill with the hedge on the right to the stile to the road (GR 263306).

2 Turn left along the road and pass the entrance to Derwent Grange (LHS) and Summerhill (RHS) and continue to the junction with Mount Road. When clear of traffic, cross the road, turn left uphill for 100 m to a stile on the right (GR 264309).

3 Go over the stile and head uphill alongside the hedge on the right. Go forward over two more stiles. After approximately 50 m bear half left over Racecourse Common, past a large stone and waymark post to a stile leading down a track in a hedge gap on the right of a field gate. Turn right in 100 m, past Wood Villa on the right (GR 263314). Look and listen for the peacock calling.

4 Go over the stile on the right, along a path through Glopa Wood. This was felled of some conifer trees in 2007 and some deciduous trees have since been planted. Proceed over the boundary stile and go forward downhill, keeping the small copse of trees in the valley to your right. Go over a stile and walk to the left hand corner of the field to join the track from Coppice Farm, left of a tall conifer tree (GR 267317).

5 Bear left to a farm gate. This may be locked, in which case it will need to be climbed. Note the communication towers to the left ahead. Turn right into the lane. This deteriorates into a track with loose stones and debris. Go downhill past Fron Lodge and Meadow Cottage on the left to a road junction (GR 274318).

6 Turn left downhill, bearing left at the next two junctions signposted to Crown House and up a gentle rise for about one mile through Pant Glas Village. Pass the Old School on the left and more woods, felled in 2007, to a road junction on the left signposted Crown House (GR 266326).

7 Take the road on the left, past Llawr-y-pant, for about 0.8 km to a stile on the left (GR 261328).

8 Go over the stile, downhill to a two-stand stile and bear half left up a steep hill to a field corner, and go over a stile. Follow the hedge on the right over two stiles and then bear half right to go over the next high stile, near the second tall tree (ash) along the fence, just before the field corner. Bear left, ahead to the waymark post. Skirt the LHS of the first hillock and the RHS of the second (which has a rock on top) to a roadside stile near a field corner (GR 259317).

9 Turn left along the road, past Glopa Farm on the right and Pen-y-rhos on the left and, by a corner, go over a 4 stand stile on the right (GR 262316).

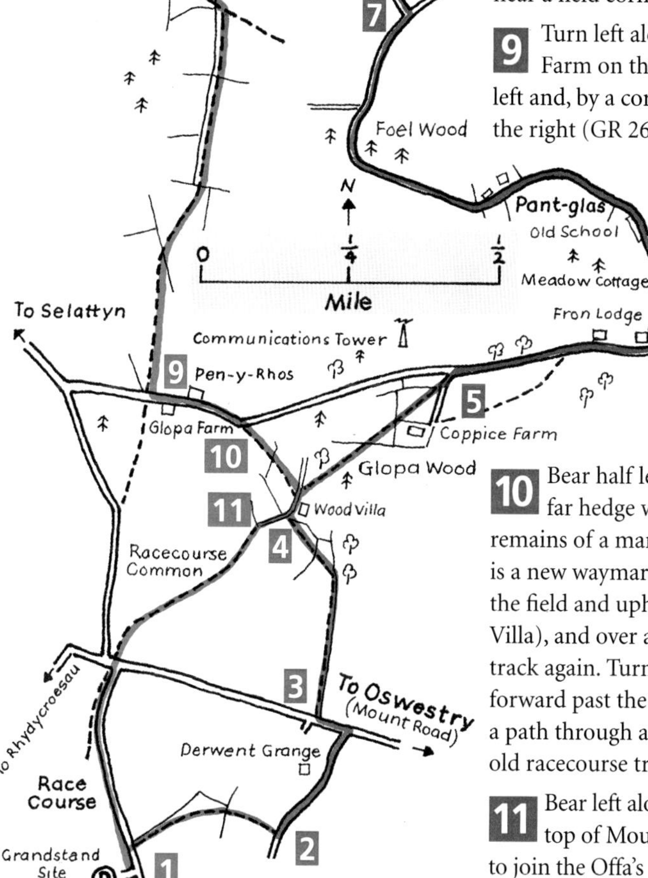

10 Bear half left, through a wide gap in the far hedge with an old foot stand and the remains of a marker post, but no stile (there is a new waymark post). Go forward across the field and uphill towards a house (Wood Villa), and over a stile to join the outward track again. Turn right on the track and go forward past the outward stile on the left, on a path through a wooded area, out onto the old racecourse track (GR 262314).

11 Bear left along the wide grass track to the top of Mount Road hill. Cross the road to join the Offa's Dyke Path, and after about 20 m bear left to the Racecourse car park.

Racecourse and Candy Woods

Peter Carr

Grade	Moderate
Map	OS Explorer™ Sheet 240
Start point	Car Park at Oswestry Old Racecourse – Grid Ref SJ259305
Distance	3.5 miles (5.6 km)
Ascent	Approximately 350 ft (110 m)
Duration	Approximately 2 hours
Terrain	Woods, tracks and fields

The first half of the walk is through mixed woodland. Superb views over Oswestry and the countryside beyond to the distant hills are offered in the second half of the walk.

This walk can be put together with the previous walk to make an approximate 8.5 mile walk.

The hilltop formed the Oswestry racecourse where the English and Welsh squirearchy held an annual race week from early in the 1700s until 1848. Before the races the road that separated the north and south commons was barred to stop carriages and other vehicles from interfering with the running. Turf was laid over the road surface to prevent the horses from slipping. Most of the famous families from the Oswestry area were involved in the races during the racecourse's history, including 'Mad Jack Mytton'. The main event was the Sir Watkins William Wynn Cup. The race was normally two circuits of the figure of eight course (4 miles). This was accompanied by 'much drinking, betting, begging and picking of pockets'. The race week included many other social events in and around Oswestry. Spectators sat in the grandstand, the remains of which can be seen on this walk, or on the banks that surrounded the track.

Directions

1 Leave the car park past the racecourse description board and take the track heading in a WSW direction. After a couple of minutes walking you will come to the ruins of the grandstand and the track of the racecourse. Head south along the racecourse past the grandstand towards a two headed horse sculpture (entitled Janus). Then take the Offa's Dyke Path (symbol: an acorn) past the sculpture and over the stile by the side of the gate to go down into the woods. On leaving the woods you will find a meadow on your left and magnificent views over the Shropshire plain including views of Rodney's Pillar and The Wrekin. Continue on the Offa's Dyke Path past the meadow and head down into the woods. At the finger post just after the entrance to the woods continue along the Offa's Dyke Path. After a couple of minutes walk you will see the remains of a dry stone wall. Turn left for a few metres and you will find another path marker. Continue to follow the Offa's Dyke Path with a right turn followed in a few metres with a left turn (GR 255298).

2 Continue to follow the Offa's Dyke Path through the woods. In 500 m you will come to an Offa's Dyke marker post with a track forking off to the left; IGNORE this track and continue on the Offa's Dyke Path (just after the track, look out for a carved wooden mushroom on the left of the path). Continue ahead for a further 600 m with the path descending more steeply now until you encounter a T-junction of paths (GR 255286).

3 Take the Offa's Dyke Path to the right and after about 10 m follow the path as it forks off to the left steeply down hill and continue until you reach a junction with three other paths (GR 254286).

4 At this point leave Offa's Dyke Path and take the FIRST path on the left running approximately level. After about 5 minutes the path begins to bear round to the left and climb slightly. After a further 5 minutes the path makes a sharp right turn and joins a drive way past the entrance to Wood Cottage. Keep going straight ahead along a forest road. After a couple of minutes a gateway onto a public road will come into view (GR 259283).

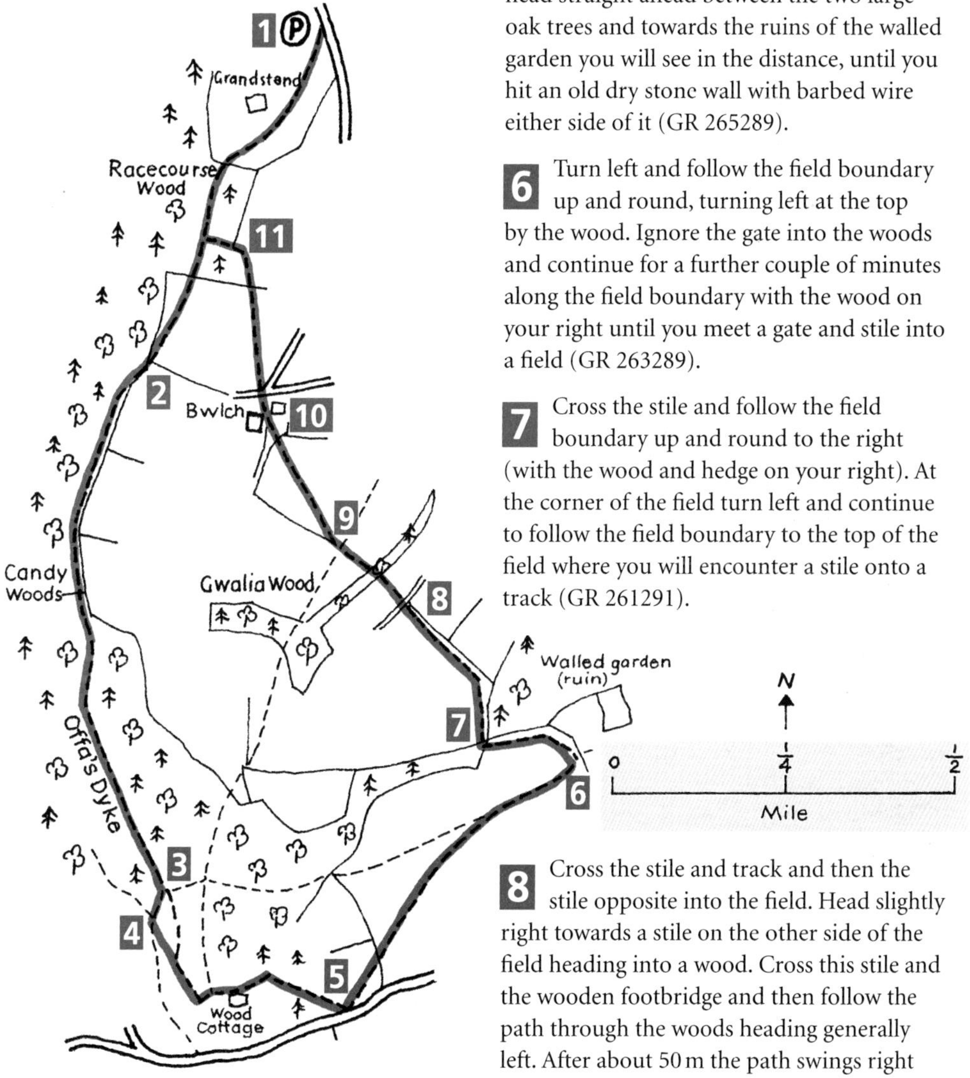

5 Approximately 10 m before the gateway take the faint waymarked track up through the trees to the left heading towards a stile into a field. Cross the stile and head slightly left to a stile that you can see in the middle of the fence on the other side of the field. Cross this stile and head slightly left past the large oak tree in the middle distance, then head straight ahead between the two large oak trees and towards the ruins of the walled garden you will see in the distance, until you hit an old dry stone wall with barbed wire either side of it (GR 265289).

6 Turn left and follow the field boundary up and round, turning left at the top by the wood. Ignore the gate into the woods and continue for a further couple of minutes along the field boundary with the wood on your right until you meet a gate and stile into a field (GR 263289).

7 Cross the stile and follow the field boundary up and round to the right (with the wood and hedge on your right). At the corner of the field turn left and continue to follow the field boundary to the top of the field where you will encounter a stile onto a track (GR 261291).

8 Cross the stile and track and then the stile opposite into the field. Head slightly right towards a stile on the other side of the field heading into a wood. Cross this stile and the wooden footbridge and then follow the path through the woods heading generally left. After about 50 m the path swings right and goes over a plank bridge and stile into a field. Follow the field boundary round to the right for about 150 m to a stile through the hedge. Go over the stile and another plank bridge into a field (GR259294).

9 Head diagonally left across the field aiming slightly to the left of the modern house (Bwlch) you will see in the distance. As you cross the top of the slope in the field you will see some older cottages to the left of the modern house; start to head towards these. At the edge of the field cross the stile (along side a gate) onto a track and then directly across the stile into the grounds of the cottages. Head diagonally right to go through the gate and then go past the entrance to the cottages up to the road (cattle grid at road entrance) (GR 258297).

10 Take the stile opposite the entrance to the road and go up past the barn with the barn on your right and the hedge on your left. Keep heading up the field and past the now defunct stile where a fence has been removed. Then a further 50 m to another stile which you should cross. Keep straight ahead with a wood on your left. After another 50 m you will encounter a dry stone wall with a stile on your left into the wood (GR 257301).

11 Go over the stile and go straight ahead through the wood down through the avenue of the trees until you encounter a broad track (Offa's Dyke Path) that you went down on the outward leg of the walk in step 1. Turn right to return to the start of the walk passing the Janus horse sculpture and the ruins of the grandstand.

Photo: Ray Groome

Rhydycroesau Woods

Ron Bond

GRADE Moderate

MAP OS Explorer™ Sheet 240

START POINT Park in the large clearing at the entrance to the woods at Rhydycroesau – Grid Ref SJ241303

DISTANCE 3.5 miles (5.63 km)

ASCENT 400 ft (122 m)

DURATION Approximately 2.5 hours (worth adding time to stop and look at the views, flowers etc.)

TERRAIN Mostly good paths and tracks, some fields and one rather muddy track

This walk provides good views of the surrounding area. In season, various varieties of wild orchids can be seen.

Rhydycroesau is a small, picturesque village on the English side of the border.

Much of Rhydycroesau is surrounded by working woodland with organic status and is registered with Woodmark through the Soil Association. This means that no pesticides are used and that the woodland is managed in a sustainable way.

The wood sits partly on a limestone escarpment. It then drops down to the valley bottom, thus giving a broad diversity of habitats that provides homes for a rich diversity of species. The main forest trees to be found are European Larch, Douglas Fir, Alder, Grand Fir, Ash, Sycamore, Sitka Spruce and Western Hemlock.

The section of the walk marked 1 through to 6 was once extensively quarried for limestone.

There are many other walks through Rhydycroesau woods.

Directions

1 From the clearing go uphill on a gravel track. There is a signpost marked 'Permissive Path'. Continue on the track to a fork and bear slightly left and uphill past a signboard. A little further uphill arrive at a junction with a signpost. There is also a small stand with a visitors book here (GR 237297). (You can cut half a mile off the walk by going left uphill at this point to arrive at the start of step 4.)

2 Continue straight on the track (with the notice board on the left) and head slightly downhill, then uphill, following yellow marker arrows. After approximately 200 m the track forks to the left (GR 236295).

3 Take the left fork, and head uphill, still following the yellow markers. The track is still well made up gravel at this point but slowly becomes a grassy track and then a path. At the top of the hill (at the white arrow marker) turn left and follow the path through the trees to a notice warning of 'cliff' and 'danger'. Now there are views to the left (north). Continue ahead to a stile on the right with notices saying that the land is open access and an SSI (GR 238296).

4 Go over the stile and turn left. Immediately there is a gate and a stile. Go over the stile and continue ahead with a wire fence on the right and a gentle drop down left. You can wander down left if you wish. Continue along the fence to a wall. Turn right and arrive at pond (GR 240298). There are newts in this pond.

5 Continue past the pond along the wall to the end of the field for the views. Turn left and make your way back past the pond.

From the slightly higher ground above the pond looking back provides an inspirational view – making an excellent point for photos or paintings. Continue to a small gate beyond the pond. Go over the stile and walk straight on into the dip between two small rises to a gate in the corner of the field. Everywhere in this area and beyond there are plenty of early purple orchids and spotted orchids at appropriate times of year. Go through the gate and walk diagonally right across the field to the hillock and to the largest tree and then to a gate and stile (GR 243302).

6 Go over the stile and turn left down a muddy green lane to a gate and stile and arrive at a road. Walk down the road for 50 m to a stile ahead. Go over the stile and ahead down the field aiming for a small black barn beyond the right hand corner of the field. Arrive at a stile and go over it on to a road. (This road can be quite busy.) Turn right and walk along to the first turning on the left before the bridge (GR 250309).

7 Turn left up a small lane (Greenfields) and continue to the first house. Immediately from the road into their back garden/orchard is a steep ladder up the bank to a stile. Go up and over and cross in a straight line uphill across a small orchard to a stile in the middle of the hedge partly hidden by small trees. It is about 15 m from the boundary fence on your left. Go over and up two metres on a slightly ascending path going right, follow the path into an open field. Keep the hedge on the right and go on to a stile. Go over the stile and still with the hedge on the right go on to the next stile in the corner directly behind a house. Cross the stile and head slightly uphill to another stile which you should cross and then go straight ahead aiming for a large beech tree and another stile. Go over this stile and head diagonally left downhill to a stile in the far corner of the field. Cross the stile to reach the road by the village hall (GR 242308).

8 Cross the road and go up the small road opposite (Ffordd Cynynion SP Croesau bach). In 50 m turn right to the Penydyffryn Hotel. Walk along the road which gradually becomes grassy to reach the wood and the start point (GR 241303).

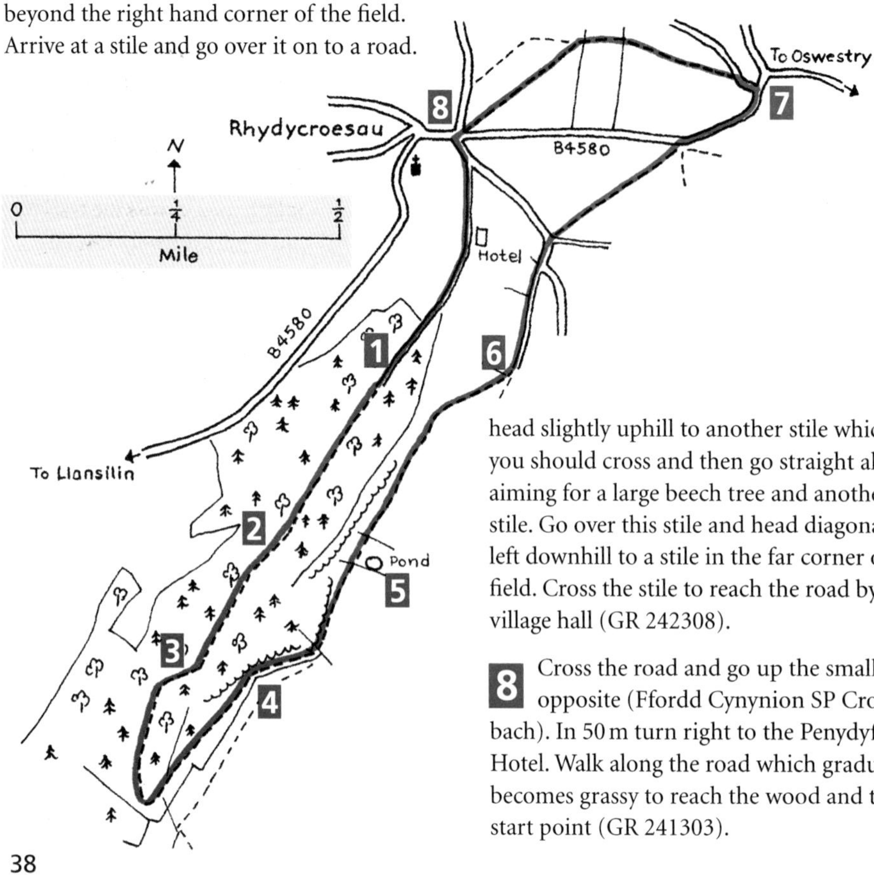

Pen y Gwely from Caemor Wood, via Llechrydau

Bob and Kay Kimber

Grade	Leisurely
Map	OS Explorer™ Sheet 240. *If you want to identify some of the more distance hills to be seen on clear days from the top of Pen y Gwely, you will also need Maps 255 and 239.*
Start point	Caemor Wood; park in lay-by – Grid Ref SJ220351
Distance	4.4 miles (7 km)
Ascent	Approximately 200 ft (60 m)
Duration	2.5 hours
Terrain	Tracks and paths

Someone said about this walk: 'All the views without the effort'. There are no stiles. However, open countryside means no shade or shelter from extremes of weather! Unless you are very hardy, it might be prudent to avoid high wind, very cold, misty, very hot or very wet weather! There are many sheep in this area. *Please be sure to shut behind you any gates you find closed.*

This area, which lies in the eastern foothills of the Berwyn Mountain range, is mainly upland pasture with scattered woods and forestry plantations. The underlying rocks, which were formed over 400 million years ago, are folded into a geological structure known as the Berwyn Dome. There are a few areas of peaty soil with extensive stretches of bracken and it is sometimes boggy.

The start of the walk is on a narrow lane running along the ridge to the south of the Ceiriog Valley, and may be reached either from Oswestry, via Selattyn and Craignant, or from Glyn Ceiriog.

Directions

1 Start by walking westwards along the road between the trees. After 150 m go round the gate on the left, on to the Glyn Ceiriog Way (marked as such on the map, but no signpost). Continue with the plantation on both sides of the path then go through the next gate and out onto the open moor. Follow the path (after about 550 m there is another gate across the track) and keep following the rough track, which bends gently to the right as it drops into the valley. This is exposed countryside, full of sheep (and lambs at the right time of year). In summer, there are skylarks and nesting curlews. Buzzards circle overhead all through the year. Near the bottom of the track (beside a small copse of conifers on the left) there are two more gates, which are normally closed, across the track. At the second gate (approximately 1.44 km from the start), turn left onto the narrow lane towards a farm, (GR 223340).

2 After a few metres and before the farm gate across the lane, turn right onto the bridleway, marked Llwybr Ceiriog Trail (signpost CT), passing through a gate. A short distance further on, do NOT go straight on through the wooden gate but bear right and follow the track, climbing steadily upwards on a rocky track towards the trees and a dilapidated building on the horizon. Pass between this building and the perimeter of the wood and follow the wide, but rather ill-defined, path near the edge of the wood. You may need to walk around a rather boggy area about 100 m or so beyond the old barn if it has recently rained. *If you are following this route on the OS map you will see that the* *path/bridleway appears to enter the wood on the left. As this path does not exist and the route clearly continues straight ahead, we assume that it was diverted some time ago.* At the end of the wood, go through the wooden gate and carry on straight ahead, following the fence and hawthorns on the left. The Berwyns will have come into view ahead of you and to your left you will see Foel Rhiwlas, Craig-yr-hwch and Mynydd Lledrod, and then views of the Shropshire hills as you look back. Go through the next gate and carry straight on. Ignore a bridleway off to your left and go through another gate and continue to the next gate (GR 204338). (Do NOT go through the gate).

3 Just in front of the gate turn sharp right, almost back on yourself, onto the Ceiriog Cycle Route/Upper Ceiriog Way. At this point you are about half way and can enjoy the distant views. Follow the track over and up the brow of the hill. Ahead, on the skyline, you will see Caemor Wood and on the left have views of the Ceiriog. Continue ahead and go through a metal gate on your left (not signposted). The path runs between two fences for a while and drops gently. You then have open field on your left and the fence continues on your right. As you reach the end of the path there is evidence of recent forestry activity and it may be muddy. At the metal gate turn right onto the tarmac lane which leads back onto open hillside (there is Open Access Land to the left) (GR 211344).

4 Continue along the lane, passing over the cattle grid. If you have binoculars with you, look out for the bird life. In about 1.2 km on your left you reach the gate at Llechrydau which you go through to retrace your steps back up the hill track to Caemor Wood and the lay-by where you parked.

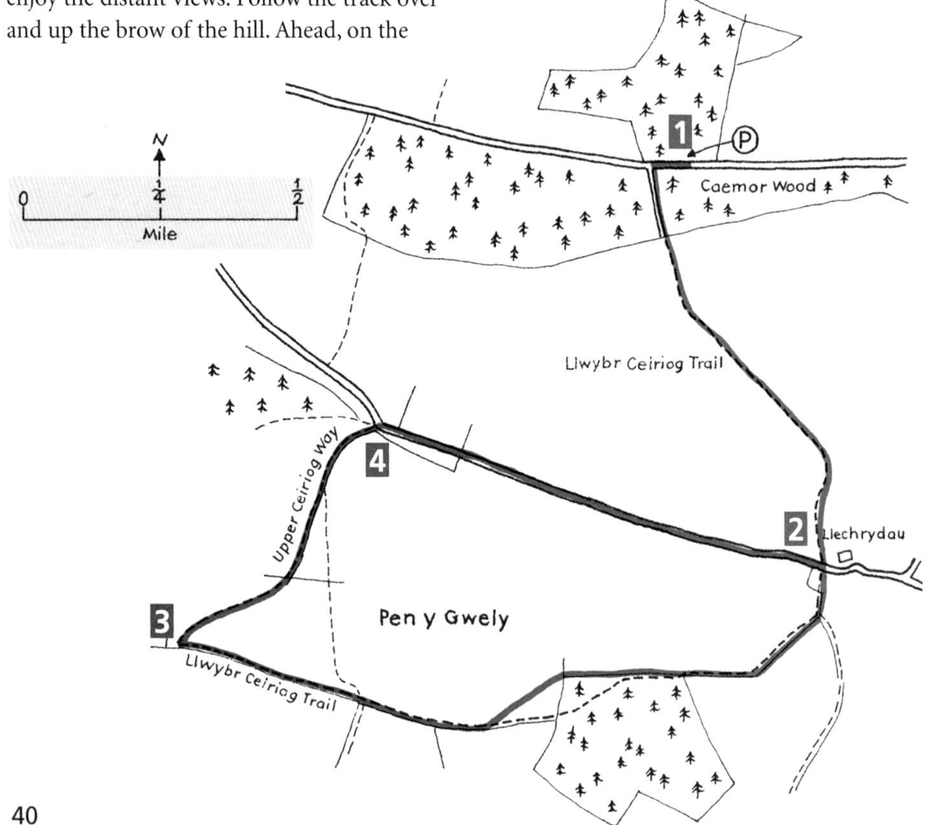

Photo: Peter Carr

Teirw Valley and Pandy Crags

Jane Hadlow

Grade	Walk 1: moderate Walk 2: leisurely
Map	OS Explorer™ Sheet 255
Start point	Off the Chirk to Llanarmon DC road (B4500) just past Pandy, fork left to Pont-y-Meibion bridge – Grid Ref SJ196352
Distance	Walk 1: 6 miles (9.66 km) Walk 2: 4 miles (6.45 km)
Ascent	Approximately 325 ft (100 m)
Duration	3 hours
Terrain	Lanes, tracks, fields and woods. Some steep ascent and no difficult descent

These walks use part of the old Glyn Ceiriog tramway and pass a glass studio, beside a babbling brook – the River Teirw. Walk 1 climbs to the top of Pandy Crags and both walks cross farmland.

Warning: Step 5 in Walk 1 can be very boggy in wet weather.

The tramway was built to carry slate and granite from the valley to Chirk. Originally in 1873 horse drawn, it eventually had steam engines. It was also briefly used to carry passengers, but closed in 1935. Lloyd George called it 'a little bit of heaven on earth' but a humorous postcard from this time claimed the tramway's motto was 'No hurry, no worry' and that 'ten minute stops were made to pick flowers!'

Directions

Walk 1

1 Cross the bridge and turn left onto the Glyn Tramway Walk (National Trust). You follow the tramway to Pandy by the side of the River Ceiriog. Approaching the village, re-cross the river on the old tramway bridge and after 25 m turn left by a terrace of cottages (GR 196359).

2 Go through the gate and up to the road by Pandy Mill Glass Studio & Gallery. Cross the B4500, turning left and immediately right, follow the minor road up through the village with the River Teirw on your left, and out to the forest. Continue on the road passing Rhosydd House to a bridle path that forks right and is signposted Ceiriog Valley Walk (GR 191362).

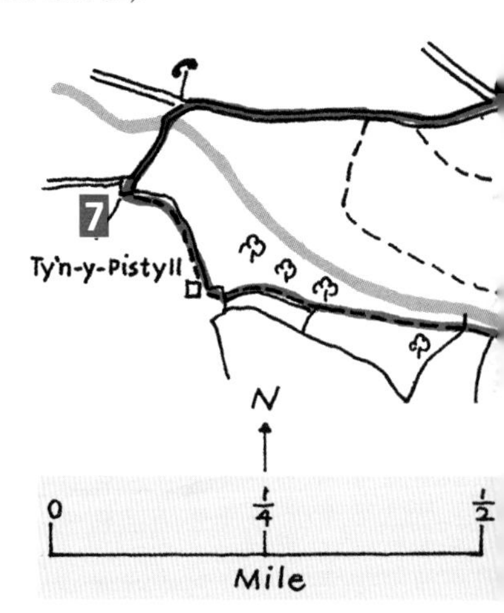

3 The path climbs steeply uphill through conifers to a junction of four paths and a notice board (GR 190364).

4 Take the sharp right path over a stile beside a gate and climb up the path following the fence on the right. Ignore the footpath sign pointing left and continue climbing to the top. *The path from here to the Crags and back is not a public right of way but is used by rock climbers who climb on the crags.* Go straight ahead to the corner of the wood passing a pond on the right. Climb over the fence by the wooden rail and follow the path through the wood to the top of the crags with magnificent views up the Ceiriog valley (GR 194362).

5 Retrace your steps to point 4, cross the stream and go through the gate on the right up a bridleway. After about 150 m take the short track off to the right through a farm gate and head straight across a boggy field, crossing a small stream and climbing to a wooden rail over the fence. Cross the paddock and go through the farm gate into the farmyard at Aberwiel. Follow the yard around to the right and at the far entrance to the road take the track on the left and follow it round follow the fence to a gate on to a metalled road (GR 186372).

6 Turn left and follow the road for about a mile downhill to Nantyr. Opposite the Nantyr Outdoor Education Centre, turn left just before a phonebox, signposted to Llanarmon. Take the lane down and over the river Teirw and uphill to the footpath on your left (second gate) (GR 170370).

7 Take the track up to Ty'n-y-pistyll and then the footpath on the left over a stile, shortly followed by another stile. Bear left and follow the track along the left hand edge of the field above the river on your left, down to the left hand corner. Go downhill through gorse bushes and a small wood and cross a small stream and then go through a gate. Follow the path across the field keeping the river on your left, to the gate in the far left hand corner, into a wood. The path goes to two gates side by side. Take the left hand gate (do not take the left-hand track before the double gates). Follow the track to the left up into the field. Go through the gate straight ahead and follow the old fence line on your left. Go through another gate straight ahead and then diagonally left following the track up to a gate into a field. Turn sharp right and

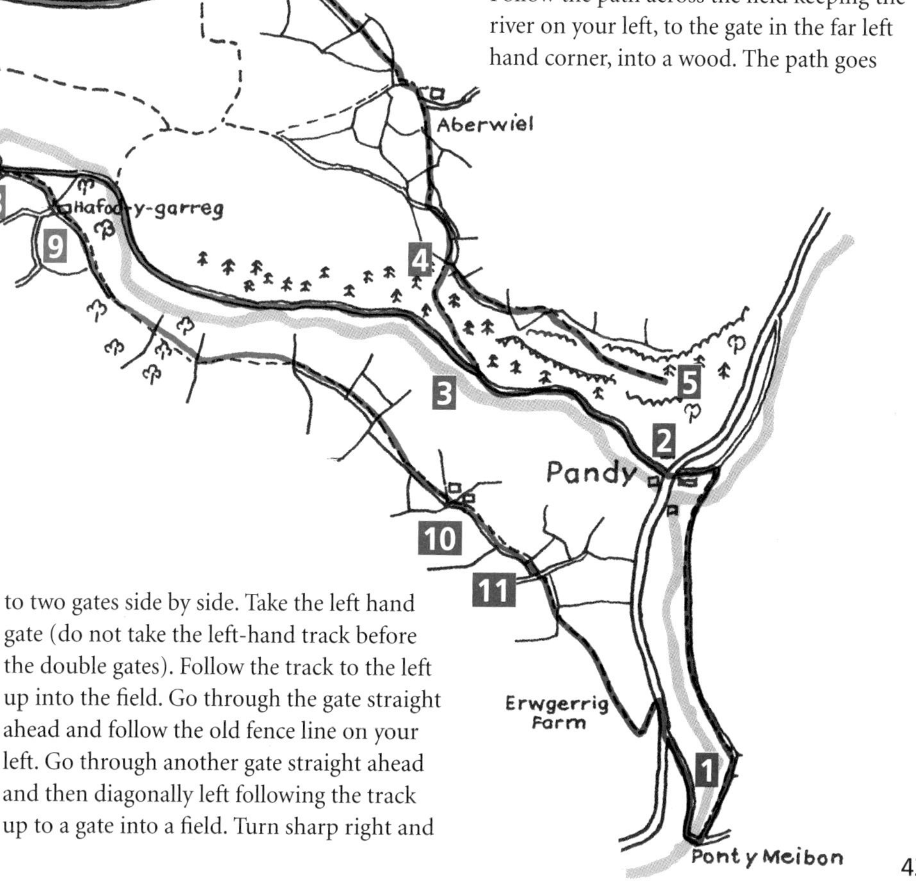

through the wood emerging at a Y-junction (GR 180367).

8 Turn right up the hill to the farm Hafod-y-Garreg (GR 181366). Take the waymarked permissive path route to the left and behind the farm to join a grass path down the hill, with a long hedge on your right (GR 181365).

9 This path leads through trees and rough grazing to a ditch, which is dry in summer, but easily crossed if wet. Veer right up the grassy bank looking for a small wooden gate on your left. Go through the gate and keep straight ahead slightly up hill. You will reach a path leading round the hill (covered in bluebells in spring). Continue at roughly the same height, to a tall hedge. Keep this hedge on your right, go through gaps in two dry stone walls and aim for the far right-hand corner of the field. The path draws near the hedge on the right as you approach a gate (GR 190359).

10 Go through the gate, keep straight ahead on the curving track, past a farm on your left, through another gate, and traverse the field with the hedge on your right, while circumnavigating the pond. At the far end cross a stile by an electricity pole (GR 192357).

11 Cross the track and go straight ahead down the field to the bottom of the gully on the left. Just beyond the lowest point you will see a stile on the left through the hedge. Climb the stile and follow the path to the left of a gate. Then go downhill, with trees now on your left and fence on the right. Go through another gate and the fence is now on your left. The path becomes quite steep and eventually becomes a wider grassy lane. Watch out for a stile on your left, cross it and follow the path down to the back of the Erwgerrig Farm, past the kennels, down some steps, around the house and onto the B4500. Take the road opposite back to Pont-y-Meibion.

Walk 2

Follow Walk 1 to point 3 but continue up the hill through the woods on this metalled road, ignoring side paths, until you eventually reach a metal gate. Pass through the gate, veering left across the bridge over the Teirw which you have been hearing all the way up. Further on the vista opens out. You rejoin the main walk at the Y-junction at point 8.

Glyn Ceiriog Circuit

George Swift

GRADE	Strenuous
MAP	OS Explorer™ Sheet 255
START POINT	Llwynmawr – Grid Ref SJ225369 Golden Pheasant car park
DISTANCE	6.75 miles (11 km)
ASCENT	Approximately 850 ft (260 m)
DURATION	3.5 hours
TERRAIN	Good paths, fields, lanes and rough tracks. Several steep ascents.

This walk circles the village of Glyn Ceiriog and provides wonderful and extensive views of the Ceiriog Valley.

'A little bit of heaven on Earth' was how Lloyd George described the Ceiriog Valley. This beautiful valley has remained relatively undiscovered. Only a few miles from the busy A5, it has retained its cultural heritage and lovely countryside. However, much of the now idyllic Ceiriog Valley was once a grim, grey place, with industries based on its rock and mineral deposits. Its main products were slate and granite, china stone, silica and lime, with kilns at Bronygarth. All around Glyn Ceiriog was a bleak landscape of spoil heaps. Attractive woodland, achieved by a combination of sensitive planting and natural regeneration, have almost eliminated the scars left by these industries. Had Lloyd George not spoken so passionately in its defense, we may never have known of the beauty of the Ceiriog Valley. In 1923 Parliament was asked to grant statutory powers to impound the upper waters of the River Ceiriog and to evict the local population living within an area of 13,600 acres. With such an eloquent advocate, the proposal was defeated.

Directions

1 Turn right out of the Golden Pheasant car park and down to the cross roads. Go straight across and down through the village of Llwynmawr. After about 500 m, before you get to the main road, take the footpath on the left opposite the Cheshire Homes car park. Go along the side of the field with houses to your left. Go through the narrow kissing gate and take the footpath leading off to the right. The footpath climbs through the wood passing a bench on the left (ignore the footpath off to the left by the side of the bench). About 50 m after the bench at the fork, bear right (there is a small arrow carved into the tree at this fork). Follow the path down to, and over, a stile and continue along the fence line to a stream. Cross the stream and go up the bank opposite to go over a stile. Continue straight ahead along the top of the field (parallel to the main road, which is below you and down to your right) until you come to a stile. Go over the stile and continue in the same general direction to arrive at a track that goes down to the right. Take this track, passing through a gate part way along to arrive at a complex of buildings, which is a riding centre (GR 211375).

2 Keeping the buildings to the right, go straight on, up the lane opposite until you come to the Glyn Ceiriog to Selattyn road. Turn right and follow the road down into the village of Glyn Ceiriog. Turn left at the Glyn Valley Hotel, signposted Llanarmon and keep on this road past the public toilets on the left for approximately 400 m to where the road forks (GR 201374).

3 Take the right hand fork signposted Nantyr, and climb up the steep twisty lane for the next 2 km until the road bends sharply to the left. On this bend, on the right hand side of the road, there are two gates side by side and between the gates is a BT pole numbered 7A (GR 187376).

4 Go through the right hand gate and straight down the bank through some gorse bushes to a stream. Turn right along the track immediately before the stream, keeping the stream to your left, until you arrive at a tin shed that will be straight in front of you. Go through the gate just before the shed on your left and turn immediately right, passing a semi derelict green caravan on your right, to the next gate that will be directly in front of you. Go through the gate and go diagonally left to the far left hand corner of the field to a stile. Go over the stile and then immediately over a stream and follow the footpath to the right to meet and cross another stream. Ignore the track on the right with the green barrier and follow the footpath along the left hand side of the stream. In wet weather this stream will overwhelm the footpath. In dry weather the stream will disappear altogether! After about 100 m the footpath climbs gently to the left away from the stream and up to a quarry road. Turn right and after about 100 m you will go past a metal barrier. Keep straight on down the lane past the entrance to Cefn Isa which is on your left (GR 194378).

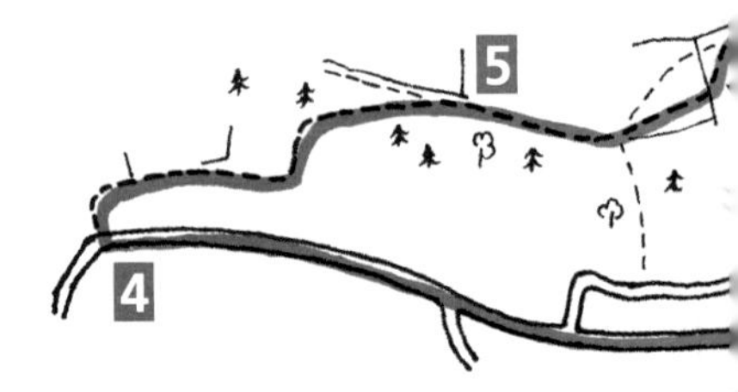

5 Go down the lane for 300 m to a fingerpost (without the finger), then bear left up the track to a gate, which is visible from the lane. Go through the gate and straight on down the track, through the next gate and turn immediately left up a steep track. Carry along this track to the end, which comes rather abruptly! At this point bear left up the bank until you arrive at a stile. Go over the stile and turn right (GR 199380).

6 Follow the footpath down and over another stile. Keep going to a gate that leads out onto a lane. There is a cottage directly opposite (Oddior Y Twmpath). Turn left up the lane (which is unmade) to a T-junction on a hairpin bend, then bear right down the hill. The lane turns sharp right at the bottom and passes some houses on the left. Continue for a short distance to a fork and take the left fork up the hill to another fork. Take the right fork along a track that runs in front of some cottages that will be on the left (GR 204384).

7 Continue on to meet a road and turn right here down a very steep section to pass a church on the left. Turn left in front of the church keeping the church immediately

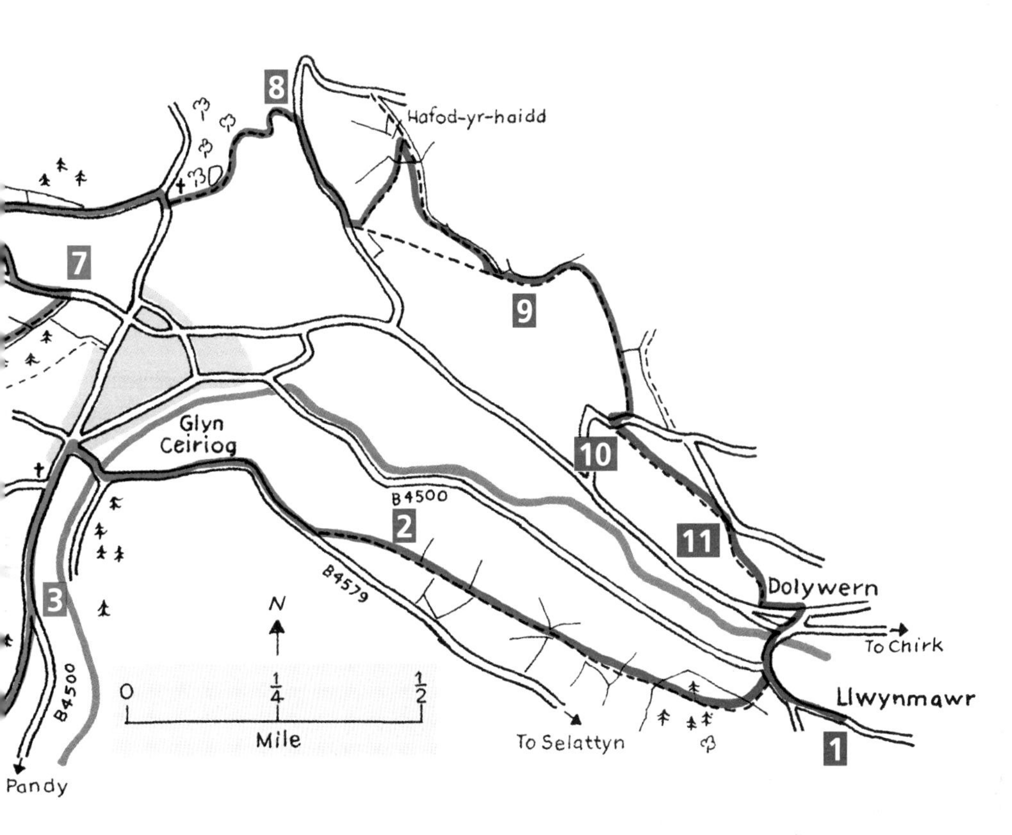

on your left. (Do not take the waymarked footpath visible just beyond the church). Cross over the stile and keep straight on towards a large circular water tank within a steel fenced enclosure. At the gates of the enclosure turn right and follow the fence down and then to the left keeping the fence on your left. At the back of the enclosure where the fence turns left the footpath bears right and down a cutting (there is a piped outfall at the top of the cutting). At the bottom, bear left and cross a footbridge. Take the middle track past the electricity pole, which will be on your right. Continue along the path to another stream over which there are placed two sets of sleepers (GR207386).

8 Cross the stream and turn left up an incline. At the top of the incline the footpath doubles back and up to the right. Follow the footpath through a gate and up to a lane, then turn right down the lane. After approx 450 m, bear left alongside a small garage. Continue up the track and through a small wicket gate. Just after the gate take the footpath that doubles back up the hill to the left and climb up along side the wall through bracken to a stile. Cross the stile and head diagonally up hill towards Hafod-yr-haidd to join another track. Turn hard right at the hedgerow and follow the track back following the line of the wall above to a stile in the corner of the field (this is the same boundary that was crossed at the previous stile). Continue over the stile and follow the line of the wall on the left to Pen y Bryn Farm (GR 214382).

9 Go through the gate and down the farmyard with farm buildings on the right and then through the gate in front of you and slightly to the left. Continue down the track and at the bottom go through a wicket gate and across a stream to a stile on the other side. Cross the stile and go down the field following the hedge line on your left. At the far side of the field follow the clearly defined track. About 50 m from the fence ahead, where the track starts to head left, take the not very well-defined track slightly to the right and head for a stile in the fence in front of you. Cross the stile and turn right at the lane and then go down the hill. The lane turns sharp left and then right between two derelict buildings. Turn left between these buildings on the left keeping the burnt out partly demolished building to your right (GR 216378).

10 After passing between the buildings, cross over two stiles and bear left to pick up the footpath (waymarked Ceiriog Valley Walk) that runs just below a hedgerow. Follow the footpath to a stile, over the stile and look out for a set of steps on the left leading up to another stile. Go over this stile, turn right and follow the hedgerow to the stile in the right hand corner of the field. Cross over the stile and turn right down a path to another stile. On the other side of this stile pass a chicken run and go down to another stile leading into Coed Compton (sign on the stile) (GR 220374).

11 Bear left and go diagonally down through Coed Compton to the bottom left hand corner to the left hand end of a row of houses. Go down the left side of the end house and over a stile to the lane. Turn left along the lane and after 100 m turn right down an unmade road with a handrail along the right hand side. Continue down the lane to the B4500 at Dolywern then cross the bridge and bear left back through the village of Llwynmawr to the Golden Pheasant car park.